# LIVE

# THE

# CODE

## PROGRAMMING PRINCIPLES AND

## PRACTICES

Essential Fundamentals for Building a
Professional Software Masterpiece

SVILEN PEEV

"We are what we repeatedly do. Excellence, then, is not an act, but a habit."

- Will Durant,
summarizing Aristotle's philosophy
in "*The Story of Philosophy*"

# CONTENTS

# Preface

## AUDIENCE

This book is intended for:

- anyone new to the world of programming,

- as well as for programmers looking for better ways to improve their code,

- but also, for experienced, long-time developers who want to remember good practices and further develop their professionalism by delving deeper into things and applying the ideas mentioned here in practice.

## MATERIALS

Multiple examples in this book are represented either through code samples or diagrams. The complete example implementations can be found in the book's GitHub repository "https://github.com/svilenp/Principles", solution "Principles", and

path "Examples/Examples.Before" and "Examples/Examples.After".
Examples tech stack

The sample projects are .NET applications, and the source code
is written in C#.

The diagrams are built using draw.io.

# Introduction

The "Live the Code" series is intended for every aspiring and current software engineer who is working on what they love. It is for everyone dedicated to the art of software development. I hope this will be a series that accompanies programmers, architects, technical leads, and all those involved in the software creation process.

The first in the series is this current book – "Principles and Practices." This is a read that reminds us of the fundamental principles and good practices in software development. It would be a useful book for people at the beginning of their development as programmers, but it also refreshes the knowledge of experienced engineers who love their work. These fundamental principles are often forgotten, ignored, and neglected, which degrades not only the software we create but also ourselves as professionals. By recalling the motives behind each principle, we will live our lives more happily, doing what inspires us in a more beautiful and sustainable way.

# Why does it matter?

To decide to study and apply something specific, whatever it may be, it is completely normal to feel the need to know the answer of two fundamental questions.

- First - what does it represent?
- And second - how will it help?

Let's start with the first one. What do the principles in programming represent?

A principle is a generally accepted rule or value that serves as a basis for various statements, processes, and decisions.

In other words, by solving certain problems, we build certain systematized practices and solutions, wrapped in a model that we can generalize under the name "principles."

And here we come to the second fundamental question. Why should we study them, why should we think about them, and why should we apply them? Actually, these are three variations of the same question.

Having a well-prepared set of tools to assist us in our work is always beneficial. The important thing is to accumulate enough of these tools and to know exactly what we have and what the function of each item is.

When we see a loosened screw, we will simply take out the right screwdriver and solve the problem instantly. That was an example of a principle with a direct purpose and a clear application.

Another type of principle would be one that defines a rule or value. It can be quite general and requires developing a plan for its implementation. As an example, let's consider the following statement:

- "Take care of your physical health during the workday."

This is a definition of the basic idea, for the implementation of which there are various approaches. One exemplary solution is to introduce a schedule and set a timer every hour to remind you to take a 5-minute break and engage in physical activity.

As a summary of the answer to the question "why," we can say that applying certain principles is essential for organizing our work, overcoming and preventing problems, simplifying things by making them more understandable, and laying a stable foundation for something big.

In software development, all of this is relevant, and by adhering to principles, we create a more organized, understandable, upgradable, flexible, and overall, more reliable code.

# Motivation

Let me give you stronger motivation to apply good practices and build clean code in your daily work.

In my practice, I have seen thousands of lines of code filled with anti-patterns, written in a rather mediocre way. Someone might say, "Well, okay, but does it work? Isn't that the ultimate goal?" Yes, at first glance, it may function as expected, but there are many hidden lurking dangers behind this way of working. Now I will try to go through most of the potential and quite real problems that *could* arise. And, by the way, they *do* actually occur in most cases.

## PROBLEMS

Let's now emphasize problems that can be caused by neglecting code quality. Some of them can even be fatal for the life of the software.

I will summarize them in 13 (not by accident) points:

## 1. Unreadable code.

Lack of adherence to standards and principles leads to the generation of a "spaghetti" code. And having such a codebase makes orientation difficult. One logic follows another, then a third, and so on. Then comes a new feature that gets "plugged in" somewhere among the existing source code. And this continues until we end up with a file containing various types of logic. This approach easily bloats the files and reaches thousands of lines where orientation becomes extremely difficult, even for its creator. Can you imagine explaining such a massive file to a colleague?

## 2. Unmaintainable code.

Every system is created with the idea and potential to grow. We should never impose limitations and lock it down from development. If it's not upgradable, sooner or later (more realistically, sooner), the software will lose its competitive advantage or ideas for such. It will start limiting its users because everything evolves, and it does so at a rapid pace. And here lies the problem: if we allow ourselves to write code like dictation, if we don't follow principles but just replace the pot for spaghetti with a bigger one, then the mess will be greater, and if someone asks for a vegetarian dish, it will be mission impossible to extract meatless spaghetti from the pot of Bolognese. I have encountered such a codebase where adding simple functionality led us to a situation where it couldn't be done without significant refactoring.

## 3. Unsupportable code.

This is a comprehensive and important point. Building the project is just the beginning of the system's life cycle. It's the first phase. From here onwards, we could have additional work like:

- Change requests
- Building subsequent versions with additional functionality
- Finding and reporting issues
- Resolving issues
- Requests for integrations with other systems
- Architectural changes for better scalability as demand and/or data grow
- Modernizations
- And more.

When different functional parts of the code are tightly coupled or have tight coupling between components, changing one place usually involves entanglement with another, and regression bugs easily occur. If there is a problem, we must first find it. Debugging a tangled code is a challenge and can take a lot of time since it's impossible to isolate individual segments. Applying improvements is also something that can cause problems at all levels if we don't have a good separation of concerns.

## 4.  Difficult to explain codebase.

This is related to point 1 – "unreadable code", for obvious reasons. Explaining such code would be confusing both for the explainer and the receiving end. Naturally, onboarding a new person would take much more time, not to mention their motivation and willingness to take on their first task.

## 5.  Difficult to document.

There are several types of documentation. To describe the technical implementation of a software system, depending on the purpose, we can have:

- Architectural documentation

- Technical documentation for internal use by developers

- Technical documentation for external use by users

- API Documentation

- And others.

Now imagine having different functionalities intertwined and collected in one place. How would you document that? And what would be the point of such documentation? If it's intended for a client integrating with your system, they most likely won't understand anything. If it's for the team of software specialists creating the product, for new members who need to be onboarded, or for the support team, confusion would be significant, and understanding would be limited.

## 6.  Subject to bug-prone code

When there is no traceability in the code, bugs are easily introduced. Additionally, when principles are not applied, we observe tight coupling, or interdependent logical parts, objects linked to each other, and interconnected implementations. In such an environment, a bug can easily be introduced with any change or newly added functionality. The reason is simple.

- To add new functionality, since there is no code separation (separation of concerns), it will be necessary to modify the working code without the need for it.

- To update existing functionality, we will again modify other parts of the code that should not be changed because the implementations are interdependent.

- If we do not have a good implementation design, we will not be able to create quality (or any) unit tests. From here, every change carries a risk.

## 7. Difficult or impossible partial rewriting

Imagine you have a project built on a non-relational database, such as MongoDB. At some point, however, you assess that the requirements for the final project are evolving in a way that leads to a relational model. You decide to change the database to a relational one, such as SQL Server.

In such a case, there are many approaches on the table, and one possible (high-level) strategy would be:

- Replace the MongoDB context with the relational one.

- Create new implementations for all Repository interfaces.

- Create new implementations for our Service interfaces, maintaining relationships between objects.

- Replace the DTO objects that transfer data from the data layer to the application layer and others.

- Create the necessary new DTOs.

- Define the connections/relationships between objects.

- Modify the mappers.

- Make final adjustments to the connecting layers between the Data Access and Application Layer.

Roughly and generally, this is the plan we can envision.

But if everything is tangled, we have files with thousands of lines, no layer separation, no contracts/interfaces, and our logic is in one place with many interconnected parts throughout the implementation, and we don't have separation of responsibilities (separation of concerns), then the solution to the task would be to start everything from scratch.

## 8. Exponential increase in the required time to develop each subsequent functionality

With each new requirement for added functionality, we often find ourselves accommodating more conditions and performing more checks. Sometimes, we reach a point where something that initially seems simple to implement becomes a complex, risky, and lengthy task due to the existing state of the codebase. Let me give you an example.

In a project I worked on some time ago, there was a page that loaded data from the database, applied certain logic to several lists of objects, and displayed the results on the screen. The new requirement was to show a checkbox whose state depended on specifics of these lists. For example, if the value for field X in list A was greater than zero, the checkbox should be checked; if not, it would be unchecked. Sounds simple, right? However, it turned out to be nearly impossible with the current setup.

The problem was that the values in this list were generated using logic that read from the database based on other logic to determine which table to read from. Additionally, there were dynamic comparisons and calculations with data from a second list, which also relied on complex logic and changes based on other dependent objects. On top of that, this intricate system had no adherence to any development principles: the code was all in one file, with multiple tangled functionalities and dependencies.

What were originally POCO objects ended up being filled with logic, and the embedded calculations became untraceable. Consequently, the state of the checkboxes was overwritten every time we tried to select them due to numerous dependent fields and dynamic calculations. Essentially, the component's state was tied to other dynamic values that were constantly being overwritten.

Fixing this situation required a serious refactoring of almost all the functionalities. We had to separate the functionalities, assign proper places for different logic and calculations, restructure the objects and their dependencies, add additional levels of object differentiation, and cover the business logic with unit tests.

This restructuring took almost as much time and effort as starting this part of the project from scratch. And all this, just for a seemingly simple checkbox!

## 9. Difficult or impossible implementation of an architecture

For example, if at some point we want to modernize the project and implement a microservices architecture, reusing functionalities would be impossible, and starting from scratch would be necessary.

## 10. Compromising security

One example would be negligence leading to the disregard of input data validations, which can have serious security consequences.

## 11.   Decreased quality of team collaboration

If we have many interdependent components, distributing the work becomes challenging, waiting time between colleagues increases, and resolving conflicts during merge becomes more difficult. As a result, the tension within the team grows.

## 12.   Non-reusable code/module/assembly

I believe this part doesn't need much explanation, as when a significant portion of our code is in one place and there is a high dependency between components, it doesn't allow anything to be reusable. Reimplementation and code duplication become common practices. This, in turn, leads to numerous problems related to changing these shared parts, maintaining them, troubleshooting if any issues arise, decreasing code readability, and more.

## 13.   This leads to a loss of quality talent

The truth is that professionals, people who love what they do, those who work with passion and never stop learning and growing, would not compromise with themselves and would not settle for anything below their current level. Suppose the environment forces them to work with low-quality code and doesn't provide opportunities for improvement. In that case, these individuals seek better prospects where they can unleash their potential and take pride in their work at the end of the day.

Software development is a creative work that, like any other, brings satisfaction to its practitioners. However, to achieve this fulfilling process, it is necessary to do it in the right and beautiful way.

## DURIAN ANALOGY

Have you heard about a fruit called *durian*?

If you have visited Southeast Asia, countries like Thailand, Malaysia, and Vietnam, then you probably know about it.

It is a big, yellow fruit. The famous naturalist and explorer Alfred Russel Wallace describes it as: *"The five cells are silky-white within, and are filled with a mass of firm, cream-coloured pulp, containing about three seeds each. This pulp is the edible part, ... It is neither acidic nor sweet nor juicy;"*.

But what is most characteristic and specific about this fruit are its taste qualities. Durian has an extremely strong and distinctive aroma. Each person can describe it differently, but there are no two opinions about the fact that it is strongly noticeable. My personal description is that it's something in between onion, garlic, rotting fruits, smelly socks, and hints of bubble gum and a sweet fruity note.

In almost all public places in the aforementioned countries, there is a sign prohibiting the entry of this fruit. Consumption in public places is prohibited, especially in enclosed ones. The scratched durian sign is placed alongside signs prohibiting weapons, for example. So, you can imagine what kind of stench we're talking about.

Nevertheless, some people are extremely addicted to its taste. It's not bad to consume it, as long as it's at home, right?

"No-Durians" sign, generated by DALL-E (images generating AI).

But can you imagine what it would feel like for someone to start consuming durian on public transportation? What if a few more people follow the example? At worst, the driver might faint and crash the vehicle.

Most likely, you already caught the analogy of durian with bad code. Even the terminology "smelly code," "code smell," and so on is used. But using this Asian fruit seems shorter, more expressively clear, and more amusing.

Disregarding accepted rules, principles, and standards is not productive in a community where more than one person is working, and it will not lead to a good result for a larger, complex, and evolving project.

It's OK to produce "durians" if you are writing some small helper module that you will use for yourself only. I often do it at home when building something to help me organize my computer desktop for instance. I do not implement complex design patterns, just because I know that this is not going to evolve more than a single class with 75 rows of code and, I am not going to include another developer to handle and extend it, nor am I going to sell this thing.

However, when dealing with the society you work in, you should switch the professional mode ON.

## THE BROKEN WINDOW ANALOGY

Another example illustrating the negative effect of using *durians* within a team is described with the following famous criminology theory. Here is a description and a little bit of history provided by Encyclopædia Britannica:

"Broken windows theory, academic theory proposed by James Q. Wilson and George Kelling in 1982 that used broken windows as a metaphor for disorder within neighborhoods. Their theory links disorder and incivility within a community to subsequent occurrences of serious crime.

Broken windows theory had an enormous impact on police policy throughout the 1990s and remained influential into the 21st century. Perhaps the most notable application of the theory was in New York City under the direction of Police Commissioner William Bratton. He and others were convinced that the aggressive order-maintenance practices of the New York City Police Department were responsible for the dramatic decrease in crime rates within the city during the 1990s. Bratton began translating the theory into practice as the chief of New York City's transit police from 1990 to 1992. Squads of plainclothes officers were assigned to catch turnstile jumpers, and, as arrests for misdemeanors increased, subway crimes of all kinds decreased dramatically. In 1994, when he became New York City police commissioner, Bratton introduced his broken windows-based "quality of life initiative." This initiative cracked down on panhandling, disorderly behavior, public drinking, street prostitution, and unsolicited windshield washing or other such attempts to obtain cash from drivers stopped in traffic. When Bratton resigned in 1996, felonies were down almost 40 percent in New York, and the homicide rate had been halved."

In short, the "broken window theory" is a concept from criminology that suggests that visible signs of disorder and neglect in a community can lead to an increase in crime and antisocial behavior.

I have seen the same thing in many teams, and it is applicable in software development. If there is a bad example somewhere in the code base and if nobody refactors it or at least discusses it, then sooner or later someone else will not resist the temptation of applying the same bad practice. The presumption is that if something that is not good stays a lot of time somewhere where it can be seen by many people and if nobody cares about it and ignores its existence without fixing it, then it should be acceptable. If there are several examples of something smelly, then everybody starts to neglect the quality of the software they produce.

It is human nature to act like the rest and to try to adapt to our environment.

Another important detail about people is that our brains always try to save as much energy as possible. If we see something easier to do, regardless of the negative aspects, we are keen on doing it. The brain will skip the thinking and creation phase because those activities will consume energy. If there is an example, then we will do the same much easier.

Imagine a software project as a well-maintained building in a neighborhood. The building's exterior, windows, and surroundings are clean, and organized, and show signs of care. This positive image attracts responsible tenants and visitors.

Now, consider another building in the same neighborhood. This building has a broken window that's been left unrepaired for a while. Passersby notice the damage and the lack of attention. Over time, this minor issue becomes a signal of neglect, and the neighborhood's overall appearance starts to decline. Trash accumulates around the building, graffiti appears on the walls, and more windows get broken.

In the context of software development, this analogy translates as follows:

The "well-maintained building" represents a clean and well-structured codebase with consistent formatting, clear comments, and meaningful variable names. It is easy to read, understand, and maintain. Developers are encouraged to adhere to coding standards and best practices.

The "broken window" symbolizes a small issue in the code, perhaps a poorly named variable or a piece of redundant code. Initially, it might seem insignificant and easy to ignore. However, when left unaddressed, signals that attention to detail is lacking.

As time passes, more "broken windows" appear in the codebase. Code quality deteriorates, readability diminishes, and technical debt accumulates. New developers joining the project might see these issues as a signal that maintaining high standards isn't a priority.

Just as the neighborhood's decline leads to an increase in crime and antisocial behavior in the broken window theory, a neglected codebase in software development can result in a higher likelihood of introducing bugs, decreased productivity, and reduced morale among the development team.

In both cases, the core idea is that a seemingly minor issue, if left unresolved, can contribute to a larger problem over time. By addressing these "broken windows" promptly and maintaining a culture of cleanliness and care in the codebase, teams can prevent the negative consequences and create a more productive and positive development environment.

# Principles

## S.O.L.I.D.

Let's start with the good old SOLID principles. We have all heard of them, we all know them, especially before an interview. And for some reason, many of us forget to apply them during actual work.

All *design patterns* satisfy one or more of the SOLID principles.

For an overview of what the design patterns are, please refer to the section Design Patterns (p. 123) below in the book.

Why are they difficult? Yes, they are difficult because it's easier and tempting not to apply them. It's more convenient to write another if-else clause, create another private method in a large class, insert business logic somewhere in the UI implementation, etc.

This way we can quickly produce new functionality, indeed. But after a few weeks or months, we will inevitably encounter several of the problems above.

So, what we can do is impose self-discipline to apply SOLID principles wherever appropriate and prove ourselves to be true professionals in our field.

## Single Responsibility Principle (SRP)

 **What:**

This is the first of the five. It states that a class or module should have only one reason to change. In other words - every class should have its own purpose and function, without messing up with the other units.

### Why:

There's a saying - a place for everything and everything in its place. This completely applies to programming as well. If we follow the Single Responsibility Principle (SRP), we will easily find the implementation of functionality X that interests us. Furthermore, we will be able to modify it without changing functionalities Y and Z, and we will also be able to cover it with the necessary unit tests. Here is a summary of the benefits of following the principle:

- Modularity and Separation of Concerns: By adhering to the SRP, software components become more modular and focused on specific tasks. This separation of concerns makes code easier to understand, test, and maintain. Developers can work on individual components without affecting the entire system. *Changing one functionality should not compromise the rest of the system.*

- Reduced Impact of Changes: When a change is needed in one part of the system, applying SRP ensures that only the directly relevant components are affected. This reduces the risk of unintended consequences and helps in managing the impact of changes.

- Easier Testing and Debugging: Components with single responsibilities are generally easier to test in isolation. This facilitates unit testing and helps identify the source of issues more quickly, leading to more efficient debugging.

- Code Reusability: Well-defined and focused components are more likely to be reusable in other parts of the system or even in different projects. This can lead to increased development speed and consistency across projects.

- Collaboration and Teamwork: Clear responsibilities for each component make collaboration among developers smoother. Team members can work on different parts of the system simultaneously with less risk of interfering with each other's work.

- Scalability and Extensibility: Systems designed with SRP in mind are often more scalable and extensible. New features or modifications can be introduced without causing ripple effects throughout the codebase.

- Documentation and Onboarding: A codebase structured according to SRP is typically easier for new developers to understand. It reduces the learning curve during onboarding and helps maintain comprehensive and accurate documentation.

- Maintenance and Evolution: As software evolves, adhering to SRP simplifies maintenance tasks. It becomes more straightforward to identify and address issues or add enhancements without disturbing the overall system.

However, it is important to note that while SRP is a valuable guideline, there may be cases where it's not strictly applicable or where balancing multiple responsibilities is necessary for efficiency. As with everything else, context matters, and the specific needs of a project should be carefully considered.

## 🔧 How:

The following scenario will demonstrate the principle by providing the "bad" approach, violating the SRP principle, followed by the "fixed" version.

Imagine that you are building a financial system for the stock market. It has several purposes:

- Help the users to analyze a chosen company by enabling them to access the main metrics and analysis data for the day.

- Everyone can make reports around that data and send it over a communication channel.

- It also provides the ability for the clients to do trading by submitting buy and sell orders.

The diagram *1-1* represents the back-end design of the features.

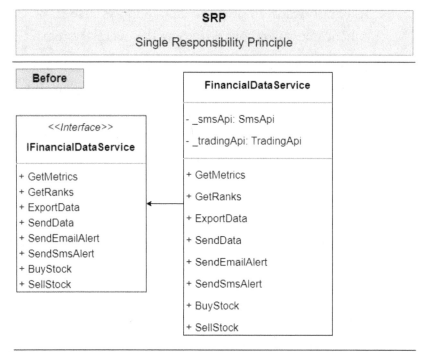

*Figure 1-1: Inefficient implementation approach, violating SRP*

As you can see in the class diagram there is one interface defined called *IFinancialDataService* and its implementation *FinancialDataService*.

The consumer-facing API provides the users with all the options that are described as methods of the interface.

```
public interface IFinancialDataService
{
    IEnumerable<FinancialsModel> GetMetrics(
        IEnumerable<string> tickers);

    IEnumerable<RankModel> GetRanks(
        IEnumerable<string> tickers);

    byte[] ExportData(
        IEnumerable<FinancialsModel> data);

    Task SendData(
        IEnumerable<FinancialsModel> data,
        string email);
```

```
    Task SendEmailAlert(
        string ticker, string email);

    void SendSmsAlert(
        string ticker, string phoneNumber);

    void BuyStock(
        string ticker, double sharesCount);

    void SellStock(
        string ticker, double sharesCount);
}
```

Consider the below list of API endpoints that are available for the consumer:

- /api/DailyFinancials/GetMetricsData
- /api/DailyFinancials/GetRanksData
- /api/FinancialReporting/ExportData
- /api/FinancialReporting/SendData
- /api/Trader/Buy
- /api/Trader/Sell

Each request to an endpoint now accesses a dedicated method. For example, consider the DailyFinancials API, whose controller class contains two endpoints: GetMetricsData and GetRanksData.

The first endpoint, GetMetricsData, returns information such as price, ROE, ROA, dividends, etc., for a given list of company stock tickers to the API consumer.

The second endpoint, GetRanksData, provides ranking data like growth potential, value index, and overall ranking on a specific scale, indicating whether it is a potential investment opportunity.

```
public class DailyFinancialsController : ControllerBase
{
    private readonly IFinancialDataService
        _financialDataService;

    public DailyFinancialsController(
        IFinancialDataService financialDataService)
    {
        _financialDataService = financialDataService;
    }

    [HttpPost]
    [Route("GetMetricsData")]
    public IActionResult GetMetricsData(List<string> tickers)
    {
        try
        {
            var result =
                _financialDataService.GetMetrics(tickers);

            if (result != null)
            {
                return Ok(result);
            }
            else
            {
                return NotFound();
            }
        }
        catch
        {
            return BadRequest();
        }
    }

    [HttpPost]
    [Route("GetRanksData")]
    public IActionResult GetRanksData(List<string> tickers)
    {
        try
        {
            var result =
                _financialDataService.GetRanks(tickers);

            if (result != null)
            {
                return Ok(result);
            }
            else
            {
                return NotFound();
            }
        }
```

```
        }
        catch
        {
            return BadRequest();
        }
    }
}
```

In the current implementation, all endpoints follow the same approach. Every controller class calls the overarching FinancialDataService, centralizing all functionality into a single place. As multiple classes use the same service, each extension or modification of the FinancialDataService can compromise the entire implementation for all consumers (the controllers, in this case). Evidently, our large class is responsible for multiple domain areas and consequently could have multiple reasons to change.

Now, let's fix this and implement the Single Responsibility Principle (SRP). By analyzing the business requirements, we can identify several functional areas, allowing us to split the service based on the type of job it is supposed to do:

- Information
- Export
- Notification
- Trading

Refer to the diagram below for a visual representation of this separation:

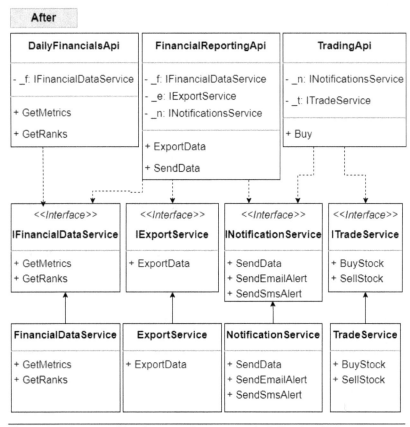

*Figure 1-2: Improved implementation approach, following SRP*

By dedicating a separate implementation for each functional unit everything will have its place. This guarantees a good separation of concerns and avoids the spaghetti mixture.

## Open-Closed Principle (OCP)

 **What:**

The Open-Closed Principle emphasizes that classes should be open to extension while remaining closed to modification. In practical terms, this principle encourages designing the codebase so that individual components can be extended or enhanced without necessitating changes to existing code. In other words, each functional unit should ideally operate independently from other related functional blocks, fostering modular and adaptable software architecture.

## ? Why:

By adhering to the Open-Closed Principle, you create a system that is more resilient to change. New features or requirements can be added by introducing new components or extending existing ones, without risking unintended side effects in the existing codebase. This approach aligns with the broader goal of minimizing code modification, reducing the likelihood of introducing bugs or breaking existing functionality.

Here is a list of benefits of following the OCP:

- Flexibility:

By following OCP, the codebase becomes more adaptable to changes and new requirements. Functionalities can be extended without modifying existing code, thus avoiding potential regressions and preserving stability.

- Reduced Risk of Bugs:

Modifying existing code to add new features or requirements can introduce bugs, especially in complex systems. The OCP minimizes such risks by limiting changes to well-contained extension points.

- Scalability:

As the software grows, the OCP makes it easier to introduce new features or behaviors without affecting the existing codebase. This scalability allows the system to evolve gracefully.

- Maintainability:

Code that follows the OCP is typically easier to maintain. Changes are localized to new classes or modules, reducing the need to understand and modify existing, well-tested code.

- Code Reusability:

OCP encourages the creation of reusable components. These components can be extended or modified for specific use cases while maintaining a consistent core structure.

- Collaboration and Teamwork: Clear responsibilities for each component make collaboration among developers smoother. Team members can work on different parts of the system simultaneously with less risk of interfering with each other's work.
- Preserved Stability:

By not altering existing code, the OCP helps maintain a stable codebase. This is especially important in systems that require rigorous testing and validation.

- Evolving Requirements:

Software requirements often change with change requests or feature extensions. The OCP allows you to incorporate these updates to the application without undoing existing work. That reduces the development cycle times.

- Reduced Technical Debt:

Modifying existing code can accumulate technical debt, making future changes more complex. The OCP helps control technical debt by guiding the addition of new code instead of modifying old code.

- Design Patterns:

Many design patterns, like the *Strategy Pattern* and *Decorator Pattern*, are based on the principles of the OCP. Following it naturally leads to applying these patterns, which can improve the overall design of the software.

- Consistency:

OCP promotes consistency in code design. Each extension adheres to a similar structure and design approach, leading to a more coherent and understandable system.

- Ease of Testing:

When extensions are added without modifying existing code, testing becomes more focused, and unit testing is much easier. You can verify the behavior of the new component without retesting the entire application.

- Longevity:

Software that follows the OCP can have a longer lifespan. It can accommodate future changes and remain relevant in a dynamic environment.

## 🛠 How:

To illustrate the Open-Closed Principle, let's look this time at the implementation of a service that provides functionality for generating an Excel document containing data for an order of some goods.

Imagine that the implementation supports several types of export based on the consumer's needs.

The *full* export generates a document that contains information about the order and the customer. It also has a header, footer, a brief description (summary) of the order, and total value. Certain styles are also applied in this case.

- The *limited* type contains truncated information about the entire order. It lacks custom, special information available in the full version of the export. The table is styled differently from the full export document.

- The *summary* export only provides a brief description of the order itself.

The ExportService mentioned above can be invoked from an API endpoint by providing the necessary export type.

The contract of this description, expressed in an interface, has one public method (Export) that accepts an input parameter (export type).

```
public interface IExportService
{
    public Stream Export(ExportType exportType);
}
```

We are going to create a class called ExportService. As it
implements the IExportService interface, it should have its own
implementation of the export (the Export method), containing
everything for all types of exports.

As there are no other methods described in the contract, the
implementation will follow its guidance and will place all the logic
and variations of the functionality inside the single function.

Let's take a look at the implementation of this interface in the
below code snippet.

```
public class ExportService : IExportService
{
    public Stream Export(ExportType exportType)
    {
        using var package = new ExcelPackage();
        var worksheet = BuildSheet(package);

        switch (exportType)
        {
            case ExportType.Full:
                SetCellValue(worksheet);
                CollectOrdersData(worksheet);
                CollectUsersData(worksheet);
                AddHeaderSection(worksheet);
                AddFooterSection(worksheet);
                BuildCustomSection(worksheet);
                BuildTotalsSection(worksheet);
                ApplySpecialStyling(worksheet);
                break;

            case ExportType.Limited:
                SetCellValue(worksheet);
                CollectOrdersData(worksheet);
                CollectUsersData(worksheet);
                AddHeaderSection(worksheet);
                AddFooterSection(worksheet);
                break;
```

```
            case ExportType.Summary:
                SetCellValue(worksheet);
                AddSummary(worksheet);
                break;

            default:
                throw new ArgumentException(
                    "Invalid export type");
        }

    private ExcelWorksheet BuildSheet(ExcelPackage package)
    {...}

    private void SetCellValue(ExcelWorksheet worksheet)
    {...}

    private void CollectOrdersData(ExcelWorksheet worksheet)
    {...}

    private void CollectUsersData(ExcelWorksheet worksheet)
    {...}

    private void AddHeaderSection(ExcelWorksheet worksheet)
    {...}

    private void AddFooterSection(ExcelWorksheet worksheet)
    {...}

    private void BuildCustomSection(ExcelWorksheet worksheet)
    {...}

    private void BuildTotalsSection(ExcelWorksheet worksheet)
    {...}

    private void ApplySpecialStyling(ExcelWorksheet worksheet)
    {...}

    private void AddSummary(ExcelWorksheet worksheet)
    {...}
}
```

You can see that in addition to the public method, the implementation has multiple private methods responsible for generating different parts of the final document. In the Export method there is a switch-case operator and depending on the given export type, a certain set of private methods is called.

In general, the entire implementation can be represented by the following diagram.

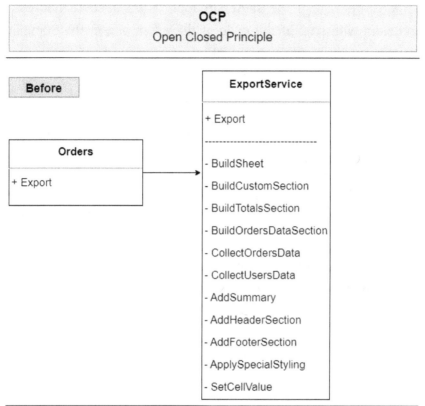

*Figure 1-3: Inefficient implementation approach, violating OCP*

The immediately apparent problems are related to extending and modifying the code base. The ExportService class contains the implementations of several export types.

This means that when it is needed to upgrade one of these types with additional logic - for example, if we want to add special styles to the table for the Limited export, we will need to change our service. This compromises the already working code. It also requires additional work such as regression testing of the entire export functionality. Furthermore, an upgrade of the corresponding unit tests covering this single method will most likely be required.

We are also in the same situation if we need to address a problem with part of the code. If there is a bug in the Summary export only, then the whole method, containing all the export logic, is compromised. Debugging the problem would be more difficult as everything is in one place.

The next step, fixing the bug, will also require changing the method and, therefore, we face the problems mentioned above.

One solution to this issue is to divide the implementations of the different types of export into separate physical places. Using different so-called strategies is very appropriate for the case. Each strategy contains the appropriate implementation for it. All of the new dedicated strategies implement the same interface, IExportStrategy.

```
public interface IExportStrategy
{
    Stream Export();
}
```

Now with this interface, we can create the three necessary implementations:

- FullExportStrategy
- LimitedExportStrategy
- SummaryExportStrategy

The repeating functionality that is needed for more than one type of export is appropriate to be separated into a dedicated, reusable and accessible place.

For this purpose, we create a new interface IExportBaseHelper and the appropriate implementation of it.

```
public interface IExportBaseHelper
{
    ExcelWorksheet BuildSheet(ExcelPackage package);
    void SetCellValue(ExcelWorksheet worksheet);
    void CollectOrdersData(ExcelWorksheet worksheet);
    void CollectUsersData(ExcelWorksheet worksheet);
    void AddHeaderSection(ExcelWorksheet worksheet);
    void AddFooterSection(ExcelWorksheet worksheet);
}
```

An example of the body of the FullExportStrategy implementation is in the code snippet below:

```
public class FullExportStrategy : IExportStrategy
{
    private readonly IExportBaseHelper _exportHelper;

    public FullExportStrategy(
        IExportBaseHelper exportHelper)
    {
        _exportHelper = exportHelper;
    }

    public Stream Export()
    {
        using var package = new ExcelPackage();
        var worksheet = _exportHelper.BuildSheet(package);

        _exportHelper.SetCellValue(worksheet);
        _exportHelper.CollectOrdersData(worksheet);
        _exportHelper.CollectUsersData(worksheet);
        _exportHelper.AddHeaderSection(worksheet);
        _exportHelper.AddFooterSection(worksheet);
        BuildCustomSection(worksheet);
        BuildTotalsSection(worksheet);
        ApplySpecialStyling(worksheet);

        var stream = new MemoryStream();
        package.SaveAs(stream);

        return stream;
    }

    private static void BuildCustomSection(ExcelWorksheet
worksheet) …
```

```
    private static void BuildTotalsSection(ExcelWorksheet
worksheet) …

    private static void ApplySpecialStyling(ExcelWorksheet
worksheet) …
}
```

Note that here we inject the IExportBaseHelper. By using a dependency injection mechanism, we delegate the responsibility of resolving the correct implementation of the interface to the IoC container. For now, just know that the _exportHelper object is of type ExportBaseHelper.

Having it injected into the export strategy, we can use its methods. Here you can see that we are interested in several of them.

The power of the shown approach is that everything applicable only for the Full Export type is contained only in the FullExportStrategy class.

The other two strategies are implemented similarly to that.

The final result of the whole revamped implementation is shown in the diagram below.

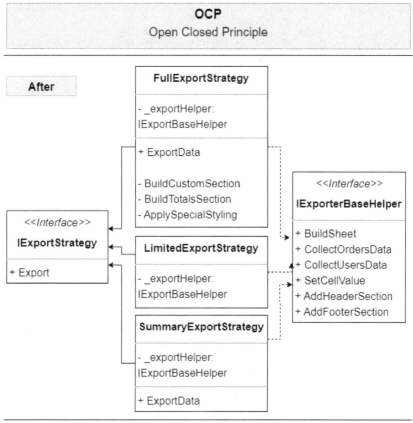

*Figure 1-4: Improved implementation approach, following OCP*

## Liskov Substitution Principle (LSP)

### ➡ What:

The Liskov Substitution Principle (LSP) states that objects of a superclass could be replaceable with objects of its subclasses without affecting the correctness of the program and with no change in the expected behavior. In other words, a derived class could extend or specialize the behavior of the base class without breaking the existing code that depends on the base class.

## ? Why:

Following the Liskov Substitution Principle (LSP) is advisable in software development for several important reasons:

- Correctness and Reliability:

Sticking to the LSP ensures that substituting objects of derived classes for objects of their base classes does not introduce unexpected behavior or errors. This principle helps maintain the correctness and reliability of the software, as clients who rely on the base class can trust that the behavior will remain consistent when using derived class instances.

- Enhances Reusability:

When derived classes follow the LSP, they can seamlessly replace instances of the base class. This enhances code reusability, allowing you to extend the functionality of existing classes without rewriting large portions of code.

- Encourages Good Design:

The LSP encourages a well-structured and coherent class hierarchy. This promotes good design practices, such as focusing classes on specific responsibilities and maintaining clear and consistent interfaces.

- Prevents Tight Coupling:

By adhering to the LSP, derived classes are less likely to introduce tight coupling between themselves and the code that uses the base class. This separation of concerns leads to more modular and maintainable code.

● Supports Polymorphism:

The LSP is a cornerstone of polymorphism. Polymorphism enables you to write code that can work with different types of objects through a common interface. This flexibility is essential for creating extensible and adaptable software.

● Facilitates Testing:

Substitutability established by the LSP makes testing more straightforward. You can write tests against the base class interface and be confident that derived class instances will behave consistently in those tests.

● Long-Term Maintenance:

Software systems evolve over time. Following the LSP makes it easier to add new features and modify existing ones without affecting the overall stability of the codebase. This is particularly valuable in long-term maintenance scenarios.

## 🛠 How:

There are several things to be careful with:

● It is important to create object hierarchies (inheritance) with care and ensure that subclasses adhere to the contract established by the superclass.
● Define contracts that allow each subclass to implement its specific functionality while still maintaining the fundamental behavior defined by the base class.

This principle helps ensure that substituting an object of a subclass for an object of the base class does not lead to unexpected issues or behavior changes.

The scenario I will describe now represents a programmatic representation of a creature living in the aquatic world. Let's call the corresponding class WaterCreature.

```
public class WaterCreature
{
    public string Name { get; set; }
    public string FavouriteFood { get; set; }
    public int SwimmingKmPerDay { get; set; }
    public Size EggsSize { get; set; }

    public virtual void Display()
    {
        PrintName();
        PrintSwim();
        PrintEat();
        PrintOffspring();
    }

    private void PrintName() => Console.WriteLine(Name);

    private void PrintSwim() => Console.WriteLine(
        $"Swims {SwimmingKmPerDay} km per day!");

    private void PrintEat() => Console.WriteLine(
$"Loves to eat {FavouriteFood}.");

    private void PrintOffspring() => Console.WriteLine(
$"The eggs are with {EggsSize} size.");
}
```

As you can see, we have defined properties for:

- name,
- favorite food of the creature,
- how many kilometers per day it swims,
- and the size of its eggs.

There are also several methods that return information.

For the purpose of the demo, they print the values from the above-defined properties to the console.

PRINCIPLES

The last thing I want to draw your attention to is the Display method. It is defined as virtual, which means that, while it has a body, it also provides the opportunity for any inheritor to reuse, enhance, or completely override it.

The process of creating such a water inhabitant is as follows:

- We create a new class that is applicable to a specific aquatic creature.

- We inherit from the WaterCreature class, adopting all its properties.

- We upgrade the Display method if needed and decide that the respective animal or fish has additional qualities that we want to use.

For example, let's create the Dolphin class:

```
public class Dolphin : WaterCreature
{
    public override void Display()
    {
        base.Display();
        PrintBreathing();
    }

    private static void PrintBreathing() =>
        Console.WriteLine("Has to breath air.");
}
```

The entire structure, graphically presented, looks as follows:

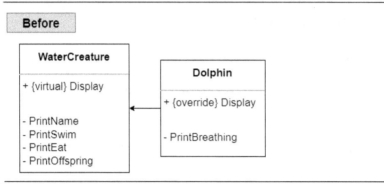

Figure 1-5: Inefficient implementation approach, violating LSP

To test the result, let's create the following controller:

```
[ApiController]
[Route("api/[controller]")]
public class WaterLifeController : ControllerBase
{
    [HttpGet]
    [Route("Animals")]
    public void Animals()
    {
        var waterAnimals = new List<WaterCreature>()
        {
            new WaterCreature
            {
                Name = "Shark",
                EggsSize = Enums.Size.Medium,
                FavouriteFood = "Herring",
                SwimmingKmPerDay = 50
            },
            new Dolphin
            {
                Name = "Dolphin",
                FavouriteFood = "Squid",
                SwimmingKmPerDay = 30
            }
        };

        foreach (var waterAnimal in waterAnimals)
        {
            waterAnimal.Display();
            Console.WriteLine();
        }
```

```
      }
}
```

In the "Animals" method, we create a list of two aquatic creatures. One is of type WaterCreature, and the other is "Dolphin". Then we display the values of the characteristics of each of these two animals.

Note that here I create an object named "Shark" from the class WaterCreature. In a real situation, it would be more appropriate to create a separate class called Shark that inherits from WaterCreature. However, for this demo, there is no need to upgrade the Shark class with anything. I decided it is permissible to avoid creating a new class and thus prevent additional confusion.

After invoking the Animal endpoint, we get the following result:

Shark

Swims 50 km per day!

Loves to eat Herring.

The eggs are with Medium size.


Dolphin

Swims 30 km per day!

Loves to eat Squid.

The eggs are with Small size.

Has to breath air.

The problem we see is that the console prints out that the dolphin has small eggs, even though we haven't set such a thing when generating the Dolphin object:

```
new Dolphin
            {
                    Name = "Dolphin",
                    FavouriteFood = "Squid",
                    SwimmingKmPerDay = 30
            }
```

That happens, because there is a violation of LSP. The base class WaterCreature assumes that all water creatures have an EggsSize property, which may not be applicable to all subclasses, such as the Dolphin class in our example.

To fix this, we need to do a bit of refactoring.

First, let's make the WaterCreature class abstract.

This will allow us to declare abstract methods that require implementation by each of its inheritors. In our case, we will make the PrintOffspring method abstract.

We will also remove the EggSize property and add a virtual method, AdditionalDisplay, to allow each inheriting class to override it. For our case, I leave this method empty, which means that it will not have an implementation unless explicitly overridden, but at the same time, it remains virtual so as not to require implementation.

```
public abstract class WaterCreature
{
    public string Name { get; set; }
    public string FavouriteFood { get; set; }
    public int SwimmingKmPerDay { get; set; }

    public void Display()
    {
```

```
        PrintName();
        PrintSwim();
        PrintEat();
        PrintOffspring();
        AdditionalDisplay();
    }

    private void PrintName() => Console.WriteLine(Name);

    private void PrintSwim() => Console.WriteLine(
$"Swims {SwimmingKmPerDay} km per day!");

    private void PrintEat() => Console.WriteLine(
$"Loves to eat {FavouriteFood}.");

    protected abstract void PrintOffspring();

    protected virtual void AdditionalDisplay() { }
}
```

After that, we create the inheriting classes:

```
public class Dolphin : WaterCreature
{
    protected override void PrintOffspring() =>
        Console.WriteLine("Doesn't lay eggs.");

    protected override void AdditionalDisplay() =>
        PrintBreathing();

    private void PrintBreathing() =>
        Console.WriteLine("Has to breathe air.");
}
public class WhaleShark : WaterCreature
{
    protected override void PrintOffspring() =>
        Console.WriteLine(
            $"The eggs are with {Size.Big} size.");

    protected override void AdditionalDisplay() =>
        PrintInfo();

    private void PrintInfo() =>
        Console.WriteLine(
            "The largest known extant fish species.");
}
```

Now, what remains is to implement the controller method:

```
var waterAnimals = new List<WaterCreature>()
        {
            new WhaleShark
            {
                Name = "Sharky",
                FavouriteFood = "Herring",
                SwimmingKmPerDay = 50
            },
            new Dolphin
            {
                Name = "aDolph",
                FavouriteFood = "Squid",
                SwimmingKmPerDay = 30
            }
        };

        foreach (var waterAnimal in waterAnimals)
        {
            waterAnimal.Display();
            Console.WriteLine();
        }
```

The result is a more flexible structure, realized through abstraction and satisfying the Liskov Substitution Principle, preserving the correctness of the program even after replacing an object from the superclass with an object from the inheriting class.

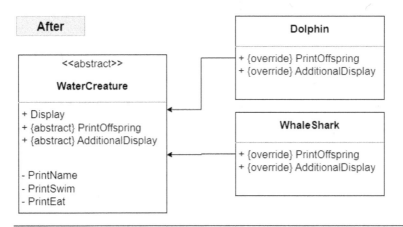

*Figure 1-6: Improved implementation approach, following LSP*

If we initiate a request to the *Animal* endpoint, we get the following:

---

Sharky

Swims 50 km per day!

Loves to eat Herring.

The eggs are with Big size.

The largest known extant fish species.


aDolph

Swims 30 km per day!

Loves to eat Squid.

Doesn't lay eggs.

Has to breathe air.

---

This time the data looks pretty good.

## Interface Segregation Principle (ISP)

### 📑 What:

The ISP emphasizes that clients should not be forced to depend on interfaces they do not use. It promotes the idea of creating smaller, focused interfaces tailored to the clients' needs, rather than having a single large interface that encompasses methods for all possible scenarios. In other words - the interfaces should define only methods that would be implemented by the concrete classes that implement them.

### ❓ Why:

Below is a concise list of reasons why adopting the Interface Segregation Principle (ISP) is beneficial in software development:

- Reduced Coupling:

By creating smaller and more specialized interfaces, the ISP reduces unnecessary coupling between classes, components, and modules.

- Modularity:

Smaller interfaces allow for more modular code, making it easier to understand, maintain, and extend the software.

- Flexibility:

Clients can depend on specific interfaces that provide exactly what they need, without being burdened by unused methods.

- Enhanced Testability:

Focused interfaces make it easier to write targeted tests for individual components without dealing with irrelevant methods.

- Scalability:

As the software grows, ISP supports the addition of new functionalities through new interfaces, without impacting existing components.

- Avoiding Fat Interfaces:

ISP prevents the creation of "fat" interfaces that encompass numerous unrelated methods, promoting a more cohesive design.

- Cleaner Codebase:

Adopting ISP leads to cleaner and more readable code, as clients can interact with interfaces that align closely with their responsibilities.

- Easier Maintenance:

When a change is needed, developers can work within the context of a focused interface, reducing the risk of unintended side effects.

- Minimized Code Bloat:

By eliminating unnecessary methods in interfaces, you reduce the need for implementing unused methods in multiple classes.

- Alignment with the Single Responsibility Principle:

ISP aligns with the Single Responsibility Principle by ensuring that each interface has a clear and focused purpose.

## 🔧 How:

To demonstrate the Interface Segregation Principle, let's revisit the example used for the Single Responsibility Principle.

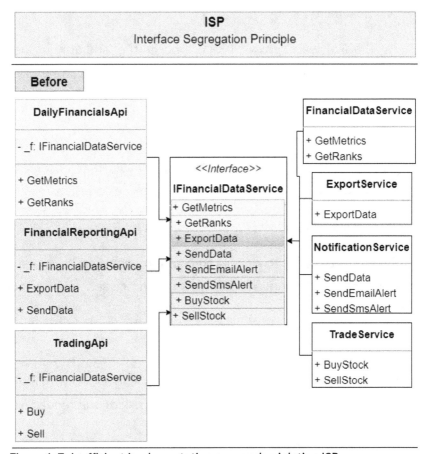

Figure 1-7: Inefficient implementation approach, violating ISP

The interface IFinancialDataService has descriptions for nine methods. As we mentioned above, these methods, in turn, belong to four functionally different directions.

If we decide to create four (instead of the initial decision with one) new classes that are dedicated to the respective functionality, we will satisfy the Single Responsibility Principle (SRP). However, these 4 new methods, each of which implements IFinancialDataService, will contain unimplemented methods within themselves.

```csharp
public class ExportService : IFinancialDataService
{
    public void BuyStock(string ticker, double sharesCount)
    {
        throw new NotImplementedException();
    }

    public byte[] ExportData(IEnumerable<FinancialsModel> data)
    {
        // Export functionality implementation will be here…
    }

    public IEnumerable<FinancialsModel>
            GetMetrics(IEnumerable<string> tickers)
    {
        throw new NotImplementedException();
    }

    public IEnumerable<RankModel>
            GetRanks(IEnumerable<string> tickers)
    {
        throw new NotImplementedException();
    }

    public void SellStock(string ticker, double sharesCount)
    {
        throw new NotImplementedException();
    }

    public Task SendData(
            IEnumerable<FinancialsModel> data, string email)
    {
        throw new NotImplementedException();
    }

    public Task SendEmailAlert(string ticker, string email)
    {
        throw new NotImplementedException();
    }

    public void SendSmsAlert(string ticker, string phoneNumber)
    {
        throw new NotImplementedException();
    }
}
```

In this example, ExportService only needs the ExportData method, where the respective export functionality is to be implemented. However, because it is obliged to implement all methods of the IFinancialDataService contract, the class ultimately contains many methods without implementation, which by default throw a Not Implemented Exception (throw new NotImplementedException();).

In such cases, it is clear that the Interface Segregation Principle (ISP) is violated. So, let's correct this.

The solution is to split the interface into smaller parts.

We saw the implementation above in the final result of the SRP example, but for the purposes of the current chapter, look at the final solution, depicted in the diagram below:

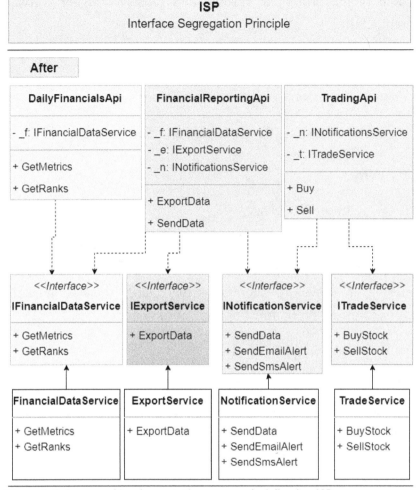

Figure 1-8: Improved implementation approach, following ISP

## Dependency Inversion Principle (DIP)

### 📝 What:

The Dependency Inversion Principle states that high-level modules should not depend on low-level modules. Both should depend on abstractions. Additionally, it emphasizes the use of interfaces or abstractions to establish relationships between components, promoting flexible and loosely coupled software architecture.

Note:

High-level modules define the overall behavior or business logic.

Low-level modules handle implementation details.

## ❓ Why:

- Reduced Coupling:

By following the DIP, you reduce direct dependencies between high-level and low-level components. This leads to lower coupling, making it easier to modify, extend, and replace individual components without affecting the entire system.

- Adaptability to Change:

When components are loosely coupled through abstractions, changes in one component are less likely to impact other components. This adaptability is crucial in a dynamic software environment where requirements change over time.

- Ease of Testing:

Components that are dependent on abstractions rather than concrete details are easier to test in isolation. You can provide mock or stub implementations for testing purposes without altering the actual behavior of the components.

- Reusability:

Abstracting dependencies allows components to be reused in different contexts. High-level modules can be used with various low-level implementations, promoting code reuse and modular design.

- Parallel Development:

Following the DIP enables teams to work on different components independently. High-level and low-level components can be developed and tested separately, facilitating parallel development and faster progress.

- Better Encapsulation:

Encapsulating implementation details within low-level components helps to isolate those details from higher-level modules. This enhances encapsulation and improves the overall organization of the codebase.

- Minimized Impact of Changes:

When modifications are needed, the impact of changes is localized to specific components. This reduces the risk of introducing unintended side effects across the system.

- Adherence to SOLID Principles:

The DIP is one of the SOLID principles, which collectively guides software design to produce maintainable, high-quality code. Adhering to DIP often leads to adherence to other SOLID principles as well.

● Better Collaboration:

Teams can collaborate more effectively when components are loosely coupled. Development on one component can progress without causing disruptions in other parts of the system.

● Long-Term Maintenance:

Adopting DIP contributes to the long-term maintainability of the software. As the system evolves and requirements change, components can be updated or replaced without necessitating massive rewrites.

● Alignment with Modern Design Patterns:

The DIP aligns with various design patterns, such as Dependency Injection and Inversion of Control containers, which facilitate better code organization and manageability.

## 🛠 How:

To demonstrate the Dependency Inversion Principle, I will create an address book API containing a single HTTP Get endpoint - GetSortedAddresses. When called, GetSortedAddresses will create 10 randomly generated addresses and then call the Sort method of QuickSortService. QuickSortService has a single Sort method that, as you might guess, implements sorting using the quicksort algorithm.

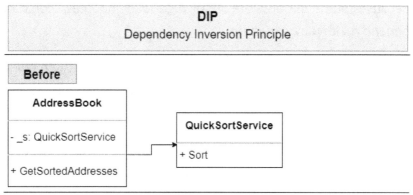

Figure 1-9: Inefficient implementation approach, violating DIP

After sorting the collection of addresses, GetSortedAddresses returns a response containing the sorted list.

```
[ApiController]
[Route("api/[controller]")]
public class AddressBookController : ControllerBase
{
    private readonly QuickSortService _sortingAlgorithm;

    public AddressBookController()
    {
        _sortingAlgorithm = new QuickSortService();
    }

    [HttpGet]
    public IActionResult GetSortedAddresses()
    {
        var addressesList = MockAddressBook.Addresses(10).ToArray();
        _sortingAlgorithm.Sort(addressesList);

        return Ok(addressesList);
    }
}
```

This implementation works perfectly fine.

However, the problem comes from the fact that the AddressBookController (our high-level module) directly depends on the concrete implementation of QuickSortService (which is a low-level module). This violates the Dependency Inversion Principle because the definition states that "high-level modules should not depend on low-level modules."

Instead, we need to introduce an abstraction (such as an interface or an abstract class) for the sorting algorithm and have QuickSortService implement that abstraction. Then, we can inject the dependency into AddressBookController.

The diagram below shows the refactored approach.

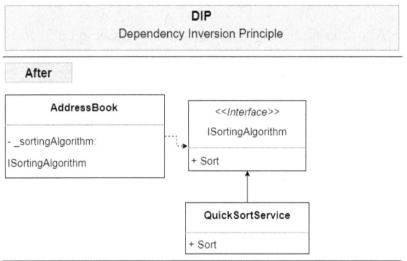

Figure 1-10: Improved implementation approach, following DIP

In this case, our abstraction will be an interface.

```
public interface ISortingAlgorithmService
{
    void Sort<T>(T[] array) where T : IComparable<T>;
}
```

Our quick sort implementation will stay the same but it will implement this new abstraction:

```
public class QuickSortService : ISortingAlgorithmService
{
    public void Sort<T>(T[] array) where T : IComparable<T>
```

```
    {
        if (array == null || array.Length <= 1)
            return;

        QuickSort(array, 0, array.Length - 1);
    }

    ...
}
```

And the controller will inject the ISortingAlgorithmService interface and resolve its implementation run-time.

```
[ApiController]
[Route("api/[controller]")]
public class AddressBookController : ControllerBase
{
    private readonly ISortingAlgorithmService
        _sortingAlgorithm;

    public AddressBookController(
        ISortingAlgorithmService sortingAlgorithm)
    {
        _sortingAlgorithm = sortingAlgorithm;
    }

    [HttpGet]

    [Route("GetSorted")]
    public IActionResult GetSortedAddresses()
    {
        var addressesList = MockAddressBook.Addresses(10).ToArray();
        _sortingAlgorithm.Sort(addressesList);

        return Ok(addressesList);
    }
}
```

Note, that the responsibility of choosing the appropriate sorting algorithm implementation is outside the controller. This AddressBookController resolves the problem of low-level object dependency.

In this sample demo project, I used the commonly applied ASP.NET Core RegisterServices, an extension method for

IServiceCollection. Its purpose is to configure and register services in the Dependency Injection (DI) container. This setup is part of the Inversion of Control (IoC) mechanism in ASP.NET Core.

```
public static class DependencyInjectionSetup
{
    public static IServiceCollection RegisterServices(
        this IServiceCollection services)
    {
        services.AddControllers();
        services.AddEndpointsApiExplorer();
        services.AddSwaggerGen();

        ...
        services.AddScoped<ISortingAlgorithmService,
            QuickSortService>();
        ...

        return services;
    }
}
```

If we have more algorithm implementations, we can create the class, and implement the ISortingAlgorithmService interface. Then we just need to register it in the DI container, and it is ready to be used wherever and however it is appropriate.

# DRY (DON'T REPEAT YOURSELF)

 **What:**

This principle recommends using a single setting, code, or functionality in more than one place in the program. This is the moment when we need to determine which part of our code contains logic that would be repetitive for the specific domain in which our project resides. When we identify such logic, the principle advises us to extract it to a suitable place where it can be reused.

Sometimes, this solution may not be anticipated at the time of implementation. However, that is not a problem because the necessary refactoring can be done when needed.

## ? **Why:**

To reduce code repetition and thus facilitate maintenance.

Having something available for reuse increases implementation speed and reduces the risk of errors.

Also, when (if) a change to a specific algorithm or configuration is required, we can apply that change in one place where the implementation resides, reducing the possibility of multiple updates and potential omissions.

## ⚒ **How:**

There are multiple ways you can satisfy the Don't Repeat Yourself principle. Here are some examples.

- You have a class with multiple methods inside. More than one method requires a certain logic. Its implementation is the same in all the places.
    - The solution would be to extract the repeating logic in the class inside a dedicated private method.
- You have a repeating logic across different classes.
    - One possible solution is to create a new Interface, and, in its implementation, you can create a method and extract the repeating logic there.
    - Then using dependency injection inject the interface in all the places where the common logic is needed.

- For a concrete example please refer to the code sample given for demonstrating the Open-Closed Principle (p. 28). The ExportBaseHelper class contains several methods that are used from three other classes: FullExportStrategy, LimitedExportStrategy, and SummaryExportStrategy.

- This is achieved by injecting the IExportBaseHelper interface in all the 3 classes and using the common logic without introducing repetition:

```csharp
public class FullExportStrategy : IExportStrategy
{
    private readonly IExportBaseHelper _exportHelper;

    public FullExportStrategy(IExportBaseHelper exportHelper)
    {
        _exportHelper = exportHelper;
    }

    public Stream Export()
    {
        using var package = new ExcelPackage();
        var worksheet = _exportHelper.BuildSheet(package);

        _exportHelper.SetCellValue(worksheet);
        _exportHelper.CollectOrdersData(worksheet);
        _exportHelper.CollectUsersData(worksheet);
        _exportHelper.AddHeaderSection(worksheet);
        _exportHelper.AddFooterSection(worksheet);

        // … the rest of the method code
    }

    // … the rest of the class code
}
```

I will give you one more example to avoid code repetition.

Consider the following common scenario:

For the software you are developing, you want to build a logging strategy where you log each error that might appear in the application. I have seen this done in many different approaches. However, many of the projects don't have any structured or established way of handling the exceptions and logging them in a proper, agreed way. That usually means that every developer would do it the way he or she likes it. Some of us would copy-paste the previous format of the logging approach, while others would come up with theirs.

Check out the following example of error handling and logging the exception:

```csharp
public class MyService : IMyService
{
    private readonly ILogger<MyService> _logger;

    public MyService (ILogger<MyService> logger)
    {
        _logger = logger;
    }

    public void MyMethod()
    {
        try
            {
                ...
            }
            catch (Exception ex)
            {
                string className = nameof(MyService);
                string methodName = nameof(MyMethod);

                _logger.LogError(
                $"Exception thrown in class - {className}, " +
                $"method - {methodName} with details: {ex}");
            }
    }
}
```

The next time when someone needs to log the error, they will just copy-paste it from the already done example.

It is also possible in other places to see a different format of the logged message, which is even worse.

To avoid this code repetition, we might extract this logging mechanism in a wrapper and let everyone just call the wrapper and it will do the job:

```
// Create a Logger extension method
public static class MyLoggerExtensions
{
    public static void LogError(
        this ILogger logger,
        Exception ex,
        [CallerMemberName] string methodName = "")
    {
        logger.LogError(
                $"Exception thrown in class - " +

        $"'{logger.GetType().GenericTypeArguments[0].Name}', " +
                $"method - '{methodName}' with details: {ex}");
    }
}
```

Usage:

```
_logger.LogError(ex);
```

In the above example we are creating an extension method for the ILogger. This is just one of the multiple options to achieve the same result. You could also extract the common logic in a dedicated service and inject this new service wherever the logger is needed.

# KISS (KEEP IT SIMPLE, STUPID)

### 📝 What:

This principle recommends creating simple and easy-to-understand solutions, avoiding complex and unnecessary functionalities.

### ❔ Why:

The reason "why" is pretty clear.

Having a simple solution will make the code understandable for other developers,

thus, making it easier to extend, maintain, track, and solve problems with it. The principle states that simple solutions work better than complex ones.

### 🔧 How:

Keep your code understandable and clean. Do not over-complicate it. The best code is the simple one. So, when you are developing a piece of code, think of all alternative solutions and pick wisely.

Imagine we're building a feature where our task is to display the properties of an object as a string.

Let's say that this is our object:

```
var simpleObject = new SimpleModel()
{
    Name = "KISS",
    Id = 1001,
};
```

And the final result should print to the console:

---

The Identifier is: 1001
The Name is: KISS

---

Showcasing our skills, or trying to make it as generic as possible, even without any explicit need, we complete the task with reflection to inspect the object, and a tailor-made formatted to primp the property names.

```csharp
public class Before
{
    public string ProcessObjectProperties(SimpleModel obj)
    {
        var result = new StringBuilder();

        var properties = obj.GetType().GetProperties();

        foreach (var property in properties)
        {
          var propertyName = property.Name;
          var propertyValue = property.GetValue(obj);

          var nameFormatter = new NameFormatter();

          var formattedName = nameFormatter.FormatName(propertyName);

          result.AppendLine($"{formattedName}:{propertyValue}");
        }

        return result.ToString();
    }
}

public class NameFormatter
{
    public string FormatName(string propertyName)
    {
        return propertyName switch
        {
            nameof(NamesEnum.Id) => GetMessage("Identifier"),
            nameof(NamesEnum.Name) => GetMessage("Name"),
            _ => string.Empty,
        };
    }
```

```
        private string GetMessage(string description)
        {
            return $"The {description} is";
        }
}

public enum NamesEnum
{
    Id,
    Name
}
```

Examine the class Before, which contains the method ProcessObjectProperties(). This method employs reflection to get all the properties of the passed object. It then iterates over each property, fetching its name and value.

Furthermore, with this implementation, we also decided that the property names need special formatting and thus introduced another class called NameFormatter, which is a method that switches the property name for a predefined string.

Although crafted with skillful hands, this approach departs from the KISS principle, making it difficult for anyone to pick up the implementation and continue the work.

Now, picture a much cleaner design - the 'After' version. Here, we've simplified implementation to the essentials, accessing the Id and Name properties directly. Any fellow programmer can take a seat beside us, glance at our work, and appreciate the neat rows, free of unnecessary and complicated fluff.

```
public class After
{
    public string ProcessObjectProperties(SimpleModel obj)
    {
        var result = new StringBuilder();

        result.AppendLine($"The Identifier is: {obj.Id}");
```

```
        result.AppendLine($"The Name is: {obj.Name}");

        return result.ToString();
    }
}
```

---

Keep It Simple, dear programmers. In our quest for sophistication, let's not forget the beauty in the simple stitches that hold our creations together. Ultimately, it's not about how complex we can make our solutions, but about the elegance and clarity that comes from simplicity.

# YAGNI (YOU AREN'T GONNA NEED IT)

###  What:

This principle advises against adding functionalities that may not be needed at that moment.

### ? Why:

Any code is a liability for the company until it becomes an asset for it. Adding unneeded lines of code could only bring problems and complications.

Here are several reasons why you shouldn't produce more code than needed to satisfy the business requirements intelligently:

- Overburdens the program. The application should consist only of the functionality it requires. Why have more than needed?

- Increases complexity. Every line of code increases the complexity of the software. If new programmers are involved in the project, then they should understand it and those unneeded functionalities will add the need for more effort and time for every person to understand:

- ○ The business logic it represents

- ○ The technical approach that has been implemented

- Increases development time

Adding more code needs more time to develop, and test, and even more time to extend afterward.

- Increases review time

- Increases testing time

- Adds more opportunities for bugs

- Increases the application size

- Could cause performance degradation in the application

- Wrong or unexpected results

## 🛠 How:

It is pretty much clear that it is not recommended to add not required functionality just because you can. A concrete example displaying this would be unnecessary. Just don't add those additional lines of code.

However, in an example here I want to show you how doing more might cause unexpected results. This is just one of the possible scenarios that can lead to wrong responses and bugs.

Let's think about writing a .NET Core razor pages application where there is functionality for retrieving user data. We implement the given requirement by creating a dedicated class called *UserDataService*.

Within our UserDataService, a caching mechanism is used when fetching a user's data:

```
if (_memoryCache.TryGetValue(
        "UserData", out User cachedUser))
{
    return cachedUser;
}

// ... Fetch from database if not in cache ...
_memoryCache.Set("UserData", user, new MemoryCacheEntryOptions
{
    AbsoluteExpirationRelativeToNow =
        TimeSpan.FromMinutes(10)
});
```

In lots of cases caching can be beneficial by speeding up data retrieval, but herein lies the violation of the YAGNI principle: the system's initial requirements did not demand such a feature. Therefore, by pre-emptively adding this caching layer, we are writing code for a scenario we don't currently need.

This proactive strategy can lead to various complications. For instance, when another developer comes to work on the system, such as when they are tasked with implementing a feature to update a user's weight (not part of the original scope), they may not be aware of the caching mechanism:

```
public void UpdateWeight(double newWeight, int id)
{
    var user = GetUserById(id);

    if (user != null)
    {
        user.Weight = newWeight;
        _dbContext.SaveChanges();
        // The user is unaware they need to update the cache
        //    as well
    }
}
```

Since the developer might not know about the cache, they update the weight in the database without updating the cached data. As a result, when the data is retrieved, it could be fetched from the cache and would, therefore, be out-of-date, displaying the old weight and leading to inconsistencies and potential errors within the application.

In its essence, by following YAGNI, we would avoid implementing the caching mechanism until a clear need for it emerges. By sticking to the required scope, the code remains simpler, easier to maintain, and more aligned with the current needs of the system. Keeping the implementation straightforward also reduces the risk for other developers to overlook aspects of the system that weren't part of the initial specifications.

# COMPOSITION OVER INHERITANCE

### What:

Inheritance is about creating objects based on existing ones.

Composition, on the other hand, is the technique of creating complex objects from smaller ones.

This principle here recommends using composition instead of inheritance.

The inheritance corresponds to the "IS-A" relationship - when you create a new class (derived) that inherits from another one (base), this means that the derived class practically *is* the base class plus the additional functionality that it holds.

- Example:

A "Car" **is a** "Vehicle".

On the other hand, the composition can be represented with "HAS-A" relationship. A new object could *have* the qualities of another object, it can be reused and extended.

- Example:

A "Car" **has a** "Vehicle's" objects and functions (like wheels, engine, it can be driven, etc.).

## ? Why:

Using composition over inheritance has many advantages.

- One example is that composition often provides more favorable conditions for writing effective and maintainable tests.
- Other benefits, which are actually the most important ones, are that it helps the developer better design the code and reduces coupling.

Here is how composition can enhance testability and code design quality:

- Isolation of Components:

Composition allows you to create components with well-defined responsibilities and interfaces. This makes it easier to test each element in isolation by providing mock or stub implementations of its dependencies. This approach promotes unit testing, where you test components individually, independent from the rest of the system.

- Reduce Coupling:

The inheritance creates a *tight coupling* between the objects, where the composition results in *loose coupling* between components. Loose coupling, as opposed to tight coupling, means that a change in one component is less likely to impact other components. That brings much more flexibility and the ability to change and extend any functionality in runtime. Composition allows for more flexible combinations of components. You can build complex objects by assembling smaller, more specialized parts.

- Mocking and Dependency Injection:

With composition, you can use dependency injection to provide mock or fake implementations of dependencies during testing. This allows you to control the behavior of external dependencies and isolate the component under test. In contrast, inheritance might lead to tighter coupling, making it more challenging to replace dependencies with mocks.

- Encapsulation and Encouragement of Interfaces:

Composition encourages the use of interfaces and abstractions. Interfaces define clear contracts that help in creating structured implementations. Additionally, you can use the Strategy Pattern or Dependency Injection to dynamically swap components, making it easier to inject specific implementations.

- Flexible Testing Scenarios:

Composition enables you to create flexible testing scenarios by easily swapping out components. For example, you can test error-handling behavior by injecting a faulty component during testing, which might be more cumbersome with inheritance.

- Adherence to SOLID Principles:

Applying Composition will naturally make the code follow the *Single Responsibility Principle* (p. 20) by allowing you to create classes with a single, well-defined responsibility.

It supports the *Open-Closed Principle* (p. 28) by allowing you to extend functionality without modifying existing code. New behaviors can be added by composing new components.

By using interfaces or abstract classes to define contracts and then composing classes that implement these contracts, you ensure that subclasses can be substituted for their base classes without changing the expected behavior, which is the idea behind the *Liskov Substitution Principle* (p. 39).

Composition naturally aligns with the *Interface Segregation Principle* (p. 50). Using composition, you can create small, focused interfaces that cater to specific client needs.

Lastly, Composition is a core technique for implementing the *Dependency Inversion Principle* (p. 55). By depending on abstractions (interfaces or abstract classes) rather than concrete implementations, and by composing components that fulfill these abstractions, you promote loose coupling and ensure that high-level modules do not depend on low-level details.

Notes:

Even though in most cases the composition is preferable, inheritance is still an important approach that has its uses. Here is a list of benefits of using inheritance in the appropriate places:

- Code Reuse:

Inheritance allows you to create a new class that is based on an existing class, inheriting its attributes and behaviors. This can lead to property reuse and a *hierarchical organization* of classes.

- Polymorphism:

Inheritance supports polymorphism, enabling you to create a single interface (e.g., a base class) that can be implemented differently by various derived classes. This promotes flexibility and extensibility in your code.

- Relationship Clarity:

Inheritance can provide a clear relationship between classes, especially when there is an "is-a" relationship (e.g., a "Car" is a "Vehicle").

## 🛠 How:

## Inheritance

First, let's start with an example use case of Inheritance as it takes an essential role in OOP, even though sometimes it is misused in scenarios where a composition would be much more appropriate.

Inheritance can be well appreciated when creating a hierarchy of Data Transfer Objects (DTOs), especially when there is a clear and hierarchical relationship between the data being transferred. DTOs are lightweight objects that transfer data between layers or components of an application.

Here's a concrete example in C# to illustrate the idea, represented by an animal base class and two objects – mammal and bird, inheriting from it:

```
public class AnimalDTO
{
    public string Name { get; set; }
    public int Age { get; set; }
}

public class MammalDTO : AnimalDTO
{
    public bool HasFur { get; set; }
}

public class BirdDTO : AnimalDTO
{
    public double Wingspan { get; set; }
}
```

In this example, we have a hierarchy of DTOs representing different types of animals. The base class AnimalDTO contains common properties such as Name and Age, which apply to all animals. The subclasses MammalDTO and BirdDTO inherit these common properties and introduce properties specific to their respective types of animals.

For instance, you might use these DTOs to transfer animal data between different layers of your application, like from a database to a presentation layer. The inheritance structure captures the shared attributes and relationships between animal types while allowing each subclass to define its unique properties.

Inheritance in this scenario helps to reduce duplication of common attributes and facilitates a more organized structure for your DTOs. However, it's important to use inheritance judiciously, ensuring that the hierarchy reflects a genuine "is-a" relationship between the classes and that the design remains manageable and maintainable as your application evolves.

## Composition

Let's continue with an example of composition. <u>It is advisable to use it instead of inheritance where appropriate</u> because of the reasons given above. If you want to add behavior on top of another object and do it in a flexible way, then composition is what you should shoot for.

### The problem

First, let's create a class called "Bird" with a single method that will represent it's flying behavior.

```
public class Bird
{
    public void Fly()
    {
        Console.WriteLine("Flying...");
    }
}
```

Then we can add a couple of more classes, representing specific kinds of birds. They will inherit the Bird's behavior:

```
public class Sparrow : Bird
{
    // Inherits the Fly method from Bird
}

public class Ostrich : Bird
{
    // Inherits the Fly method from Bird, but ostriches can't fly!
    // Override the Fly method and throw an exception
    public new void Fly()
    {
        throw new InvalidOperationException(
        "Ostriches can't fly!");
    }
}
```

You can see the problem with this approach illustrated above. In case of a non-flying bird, like the ostrich, the flying function is not applicable, so we are overriding that method and throwing an exception. This is not the best thing we can do in such situations, so let's refactor this code by using composition.

## The solution

```
public interface IFlyBehavior
{
    void Fly();
}

public class FlyWithWings : IFlyBehavior
{
    public void Fly()
    {
        Console.WriteLine("Flying...");
    }
}

public class NoFly : IFlyBehavior
{
    public void Fly()
    {
        Console.WriteLine("Can't fly...");
    }
}

public class Bird
{
    private readonly IFlyBehavior _flyBehavior;

    public Bird(IFlyBehavior flyBehavior)
    {
        _flyBehavior = flyBehavior;
    }

    public void PerformFly()
    {
        _flyBehavior.Fly();
    }
}

public class Sparrow : Bird
{
    public Sparrow() : base(new FlyWithWings())
    {
```

```
        // Sparrow can fly so we use FlyWithWings behavior
    }
}
public class Ostrich : Bird
{
    public Ostrich() : base(new NoFly())
    {
        // Ostrich can't fly so we use NoFly behavior
    }
}
```

In the composition example, we define a Bird class that has a behavior for flying (IFlyBehavior) as a private member. It's composed of a fly behavior instead of inheriting from a base class. We can then create specific implementations of the IFlyBehavior for flying and not flying, delegating the task of flying to the behavior classes.

The Sparrow class is composed of the FlyWithWings behavior indicating that the sparrow can fly. On the other hand, the Ostrich class is composed of the NoFly behavior because ostriches can't fly. This way, each bird class only has the behaviors it needs, and we avoid the problem of having to override inherited methods that don't make sense for some subclasses. We can also add, remove, or change the fly behavior dynamically at runtime if we want to, giving us more flexibility.

# CONVENTION OVER CONFIGURATION (COC)

### What:

This principle recommends using conventions for settings and file and folder naming instead of explicitly configuring everything.

## ? Why:

The "Convention over Configuration" principle in software development is a design philosophy that advocates defaulting to predefined conventions rather than requiring explicit configuration for every aspect of a system. Here's why using the CoC can be beneficial:

- Reduced Complexity:

CoC reduces the need for developers to make extensive configuration decisions, simplifying the setup process and making it easier to start new projects.

- Consistency:

By following consistent conventions, developers create a common structure that promotes a shared understanding of code and project organization across the team.

- Faster Development:

CoC can accelerate development by minimizing time spent on repetitive configuration tasks, enabling developers to focus on implementing actual features.

- Ease of Onboarding:

New team members can quickly get up to speed by following established conventions, reducing the learning curve.

- Less Error-Prone:

CoC reduces the likelihood of configuration errors and inconsistencies, leading to more reliable and predictable outcomes.

- Standardization:

Conventions set a standard for how various components are named, organized, and interact, making it easier to integrate and maintain different parts of the system.

- Implicit Documentation:

Conventions act as implicit documentation, making code easier to understand without requiring extensive comments or explanations.

- Community and Tools:

Many frameworks and libraries leverage CoC, which leads to a more seamless integration of third-party tools and libraries.

- Focus on Business Logic:

Developers can focus on writing business logic rather than spending time configuring low-level settings.

- Rapid Prototyping:

CoC is particularly valuable during rapid prototyping or early project stages when quick development and iterations are crucial.

- Less Decision Fatigue:

With default conventions, developers don't need to make as many configuration decisions, reducing decision fatigue and promoting quicker decision-making on more critical matters.

- Maintainability:

CoC can lead to more maintainable codebases, as the standardized structure makes it easier for developers to locate and modify code.

While CoC offers numerous advantages, it's essential to strike a balance. Conventions should be chosen thoughtfully, considering the project's context and the team's needs. In situations where specific configurations are necessary, CoC can be complemented by configuration options that allow flexibility when needed.

## 🔧 How:

In Entity Framework Core (EF Core), the Code First approach is a prime example of Convention over Configuration. It automatically maps object names (classes and properties) to database tables and columns, significantly reducing the need for explicit configuration.

Let's assume we want to create a simple data model for a blog application with two entities: Post and Author. We'll create classes to represent these entities, and EF Core will infer the table names and relationships based on naming conventions.

```
using Microsoft.EntityFrameworkCore;

namespace BlogApp.Models
{
    public class BlogContext : DbContext
    {
        public DbSet<Post> Posts { get; set; }
        public DbSet<Author> Authors { get; set; }

        protected override void
OnConfiguring(DbContextOptionsBuilder optionsBuilder)
        {
            optionsBuilder.UseSqlServer("connection_string_here");
        }
    }

    public class Post
    {
        public int Id { get; set; }
        public string Title { get; set; }
        public string Content { get; set; }

        // Relationship with Author
        public int AuthorId { get; set; }
```

```
        public Author Author { get; set; }
    }

    public class Author
    {
        public int Id { get; set; }
        public string Name { get; set; }

        // Navigation property for related Posts
        public List<Post> Posts { get; set; }
    }
}
```

In the above code:

We have defined two classes, Post and Author, to represent the data model. The properties within each class will be mapped to columns in the corresponding database table.

We set up a DbContext class named BlogContext. The DbContext is the bridge between the application and the database. Here, we define the database sets Posts and Authors, representing the respective database tables.

We have a single line of configuration within the OnConfiguring method to specify the database connection string. The rest of the configurations are inferred through naming conventions.

Convention over Configuration in EF Core:

EF Core uses naming conventions to map object names to database tables and columns automatically.

For example, the class name Post will be mapped to the database table named "Posts."

The property Id in the Post class will be recognized as the primary key for the "Posts" table.

The AuthorId property in the Post class will be identified as a foreign key referencing the "Authors" table.

Likewise, the Author class and its properties will be mapped to the "Authors" table and columns.

By following these naming conventions, EF Core simplifies the configuration process. Developers don't need to specify explicit table or column names, primary keys, or foreign keys. Instead, the framework automatically handles these configurations based on the class and property names, allowing for a streamlined and efficient development experience.

# SEPARATION OF CONCERNS

### 📝 What:

This principle recommends separating the program into components that handle specific functionalities or aspects.

### ❓ Why:

Having a dedicated place per functional area brings order, better and faster maintenance, easier and much safer growth and evolution of the project, and testability.

### 🔧 How:

We already covered the topic under the SOLID principles, and to be more precise, the Single Responsibility and Open-Closed Principles are primarily those that satisfy the separation of concerns principle.

By adhering to the Single Responsibility Principle, we ensure that each class is focused on a specific task or functionality. This separation of concerns helps maintain code readability, reusability, and maintainability. When a class has multiple responsibilities, changes to one part of the class can inadvertently affect other unrelated parts, leading to tightly coupled and brittle code.

To achieve the Separation of Concerns, it is essential to identify distinct responsibilities within a system and assign each responsibility to separate classes or modules. This allows for better code organization and reduces the risk of unintended side effects when making changes or extending the system.

From the above sections, you already know that the Open/Closed Principle states that software entities (such as classes, modules, or functions) should be open for extension but closed for modification. In other words, once a module or class is developed and tested, its implementation should not be modified when extending the system's functionality. Instead, new functionality should be added through extensions or subclassing, without altering the existing code.

When you separate concerns by following the Single Responsibility Principle (SRP) and creating smaller, focused modules or classes, it becomes easier to adhere to the Open/Closed Principle. Each module or class is responsible for a specific concern. When you need to extend the system's functionality, you can create new classes or modules without modifying the existing ones.

By combining the Separation of Concerns with the Open/Closed Principle, you achieve a more maintainable and extensible codebase. When a system is well-separated into smaller, coherent components, it's easier to understand, maintain, and modify. When new requirements arise, you can extend the system by introducing new components or classes rather than modifying existing ones, reducing the risk of introducing bugs or unintended side effects.

In summary, both, the Single Responsibility Principle and the Open/Closed Principle are relevant to achieving Separation of Concerns and contribute to building maintainable and extensible software systems. They work together to create a modular and flexible architecture that promotes code reuse and easier maintenance.

## BORROW AND IMPROVE

### What:

This is probably one of the most useful principles not only in the software development area but practically for anything. Its concept is simple - use something existing, something known, and apply it to accomplish an idea of yours by adapting it to your needs. During the adaptation process, you can improve it and make it even more useful, performant, and suitable for the concrete use case.

### Why:

To save time and effort for brainstorming, testing, and development from scratch and all the risks associated with those processes.

### How:

Like any other artistic and creative profession, in software development, it is a common practice to "steal" ideas. Please interpret it in the most positive connotation. Reusing an already existing implementation is something that every developer should master and practically do.

Here is the first point of the practical implementation of the "Borrow and Improve" principle:

   **1.** Read *a lot*.

Reading books, articles, blog posts, comments in a community or a group, magazines. Read as much as you can from specialized literature that you can access. This is one of the most important parts of becoming good in your field and being able to apply the "Borrow and Improve" principle.

Be constantly exposed to information, examples, best practices, and solutions to all kinds of problems in the software development world. Only that way you will "Live the code". That is how you will always have different options for solving specific problems in your head.

It is not required, and not possible, to remember everything. However, constantly exposing yourself to information affects your brain (*mostly* positively). You start to link the information you already have, with the new data and thus form new neural networks. Doing that will literally make you smarter and have a better arsenal of tools in your head.

You will also enrich your subconscious which will help you with automatic decision-making in future events.

I'll finish this point with a quote from Charles T. Munger, an American business magnate, lawyer, investor, and philanthropist. Until his death on Nov 28, 2023, he was Vice-Chairman of Berkshire Hathaway Corporation, the diversified investment corporation chaired by Warren Buffett. He is also known as the right-hand of Buffett. Here is what he says:

"In my whole life, I have known no wise people (over a broad subject matter area) who didn't read all the time -- none, zero. You'd be amazed at how much Warren reads--and at how much I read. My children laugh at me. They think I'm a book with a couple of legs sticking out."

The purpose is to apply in practice different strategies you have read about or have seen.

**2.** Experiment.

If you apply point 1 (Read *a lot*), which, remember, is a never-ending thing, then you will have a pretty good library of options in your brain. You will know that there are multiple solutions available for solving dedicated problems. It is enough to be aware about their existence and the main concept. Don't worry about the concrete implementation. This is something you can research when you pick one.

Let's take the following example to illustrate the idea:

- Requirements

Imagine you work for a company that makes protein bars. The software you are developing is meant to build the final ingredients label on the package. The requirements for generating this ingredient statement text are based on the following:

  o Make the ingredients in the ingredients list text to be comma-separated, starting with the word "Contains:", based on the below criteria.

- o Include all nuts in the final product that constitute more than 3% of the bar recipe.

- o Include all fruits in the final product that constitute more than 5% of the bar recipe.

- o Include all types of powders (e.g., protein powder, maca powder, cocoa powder).

- o Include the sugar content.

- o Include all other ingredients that weigh more than 0.05 grams per 100 grams of the product.

- o Order the ingredients by weight in descending order.

- o Capitalize the first letter of each ingredient.

- o Identify and mark all allergens from a predefined list in bold.

- o On a new line at the end of the text, include the final protein content in percentage using the format: (Protein: [percentage]%).

Example output text:

Contains: Dates, Mango, Cashew nuts, **Soy** protein powder, **Whey** protein powder, Sugar (2g), Maltitol, Flax seed.

Protein: 22%.

- • Design and implementation (the *Borrow* part)

Hopefully, you will not go with a spaghetti monolith single-class implementation. Let's build an elegant and useful code base instead.

Obviously, the requirement speaks about generating a text, by extracting different kinds of data from several sources, applying business logic, then modifying this text, applying more logic, and modifying it again. In the end, it is concatenated with another logical piece.

Now, using your brain library, you will come up with several options. Probably the first thing you will remember about such scenarios with *multi-step process implementation* is a design pattern called *"Chain of Responsibility"*. And that is enough! Now you have hundreds of sources to examine in detail the mentioned design pattern and implement it in your solution.

- Refinement (the *Improvement* part)

You have the initial idea and have started the implementation. The next step is to adapt it to your specific needs. There are many example implementations available, and you will likely choose one to modify. During the adaptation process, you can integrate additional design patterns and apply best practices.

Following is one option to achieve this.

- Modular Design: Create an interface to describe the extraction of ingredient data. This interface can have several implementations, each handling a specific category (e.g., fruits, nuts, powders).

- Factory Pattern: Apply the factory pattern to select the appropriate implementation based on the ingredient type.

- Chain of Responsibility: Use the Chain of Responsibility pattern combined with the Strategy pattern. This allows each handler in the chain to use a different strategy for processing the specific steps.

So, you will refine the initial idea and make it even better. Doing so enhances flexibility, maintainability, and scalability, achieving the goal of improving the original concept. That is the purpose of the given principle.

# THE DISCOVERER

### 📑 What:

It is about developing a particular pattern, algorithm, or framework to address a certain problem. The idea is to create a solution that not only defines the problem's specifics but can also be ideally reused in similar contexts.

### ❓ Why:

Being creative and innovative has a huge impact on our personality. When we invent something useful, there are side effects of increasing self-satisfaction, self-confidence, self-esteem, and an overall feel-good mood.

This could push us further in our careers and could inspire the people we are working with.

### 🛠 How:

This can be one variation of the previous principle "Borrow and Improve". When you extend, modify, and fine-tune the thing that you have "borrowed", it can become something new.

To create this invention, you need to:

- Add a structure.

- Create the appropriate abstraction and make it generic enough.

- Refine it even more by making it clear and understandable.

- Describe the approach by creating appropriate documentation and example usage.

- Add code snippets and guidance.

- Popularize your creation.

# THE HISTORIAN

### What:

This approach stands for re-using well-established, documented solutions for common problems. It aligns well with good software development practices. *The Historian* emphasizes learning from past experiences, adopting well-established solutions, and leveraging historical knowledge to improve efficiency and effectiveness.

### Why:

Lots of people have already been struggling with some design or implementation problems through the years and even though the technology changes, some basic ideas stay forever, since they are kind of a foundation.

Knowing the history of software development and implementing the advised techniques could be very valuable for the following reasons:

- Efficiency:

Learning from historical solutions and best practices reduces the need to reinvent the wheel. This efficiency accelerates development by avoiding unnecessary trial and error.

- Quality Improvement:

Relying on proven approaches enhances the quality of the solution. Solutions that have stood the test of time are more likely to be robust and reliable.

- Time Savings:

By adopting established techniques, you save time that would otherwise be spent exploring uncharted territory or dealing with unforeseen challenges.

- Risk Reduction:

Solutions that have been used successfully in the past reduce the risk of encountering unexpected problems, contributing to smoother development and more predictable outcomes.

- Shared Knowledge:

Adopting well-known techniques promotes a shared vocabulary and understanding among team members, facilitating communication and collaboration.

- Long-Term Maintenance:

Solutions rooted in history are often easier to maintain over time, as they align with established best practices and are less prone to becoming outdated quickly.

- Learning Opportunity:

Exploring historical solutions can be educational, providing insights into the evolution of software development and the reasoning behind certain design choices.

- Consistency:

Using established techniques fosters consistency across projects, making it easier to transition between different projects and codebases.

- Building on Experience:

By building on the collective experience of the software development community, you benefit from the insights and lessons learned by those who have tackled similar challenges.

Note:

While the Historian principle is valuable, it's also important to balance leveraging existing knowledge and innovating when necessary. Sometimes, new challenges require unique approaches.

## 🛠 How:

Applying "The Historian" principle involves incorporating well-established, documented solutions and techniques into your software development process. Here's how you can put this principle into practice:

- Research and Study:

Regularly invest time in researching and studying established practices, design patterns, and frameworks that have been successful in addressing common software development challenges.

- Documented Solutions:

Seek out reputable sources of documentation, books, articles, and tutorials that provide insights into proven solutions and techniques. These resources often provide valuable historical context.

- Best Practice Adoption:

Identify industry-recognized best practices and incorporate them into your development workflow. These practices have stood the test of time and will likely bring efficiency and quality to your projects.

- Community Involvement:

Participate in developer communities, forums, and conferences where experienced developers share their knowledge and insights. Engaging in discussions and learning from others' experiences can be invaluable.

- Standard Libraries and Frameworks:

Leverage well-maintained and widely used libraries, frameworks, and tools. These tools have often been refined over time and can significantly speed up development while ensuring reliability.

- Mentoring and Collaboration:

Encourage mentoring and collaboration within your team. Experienced team members can share their historical knowledge with less-experienced developers. That is a win-win strategy promoting mutual learning.

For example, you can study the Gang of Four design patterns (please, refer to the chapter <u>Design Patterns </u>(p. 123) for a brief overview of what they are in a high-level description).

# THE GOOD BOY SCOUT

###  What:

It advises to leave the codebase in a better state than you found it. The Good Boy Scout Principle is about promoting code hygiene and maintainability. It suggests that whenever a developer works on a piece of code, they should make small improvements, clean up any mess or inconsistencies, and ensure that the code is well-documented and follows best practices. The goal is to get rid of any *durians* from the code base if you encounter such.

### ? Why:

- **Continuous Improvement**: Applying the Good Boy Scout Principle fosters a culture of continuous improvement within a development team. It ensures the codebase doesn't accumulate technical debt, making it easier to maintain and extend over time.
- **Enhanced Collaboration**: Cleaner and more organized code is easier for other team members to understand and work with. It improves collaboration, as team members can quickly grasp the code's intent and make changes without fear of introducing errors.
- **Reduced Debugging Time**: Well-maintained code is less likely to contain bugs or inconsistencies. By adhering to this principle, developers reduce the time spent debugging and fixing issues in the future.

## 🔧 How:

To apply this principle, you have to adopt the correct mindset. Several things will help with that.

When you provide improvements and contribute to the team with quality and efficient work your body typically experiences a positive emotional response. This positive emotional response can lead to the release of several hormones, including:

- *Dopamine*: Often referred to as the "feel-good" hormone, dopamine is released when you experience pleasure and satisfaction. It plays a significant role in the brain's reward system. Achieving a goal or seeing positive results from your work can trigger dopamine release.

- *Serotonin*: Serotonin is associated with feelings of well-being and happiness. When you accomplish tasks and feel a sense of pride or recognition from your team or peers, serotonin levels can increase.

- *Endorphins*: Endorphins are natural painkillers produced by the body. They're released during strenuous physical activity, stress, and even moments of accomplishment. Achieving a goal or seeing positive results can trigger endorphin release and create a sense of euphoria.

- *Oxytocin*: Often called the "bonding hormone" or "love hormone," oxytocin is released during social interactions and positive connections with others. When your team celebrates a successful project, achievement, or improvement of any kind, oxytocin levels can rise as you feel a sense of camaraderie and connection.

These hormones work together to reinforce the positive feelings associated with achieving goals, working efficiently, and receiving recognition for your efforts. They can motivate you to continue performing well and foster a sense of teamwork and collaboration within the group.

Furthermore, when you apply this principle and always go the extra mile by improving someone else's work with no concrete task, you will constantly make a positive impression on your colleagues and also on your superiors. That will help you to be an important employee and probably will move you ahead for a promotion.

The next step is to *be vigilant*.

When you are working on a task on a common project, you will go through an already created code base, developed by a coworker or maybe by yourself. So the idea is to look for everything that you think should be fixed or improved, even if it is not your responsibility at that particular moment.

The final step is to take responsibility and *make improvements*.

The hard thing is that it seems that you need to do it "for free". This is an extra effort for you, and extra time you need to spend to do something you are not asked for. The truth is that those things will be seen and felt, and you will be rewarded for it.

I have one extra step:

*Educate* the team members. Promote awareness of the Good Boy Scout Principle within the team, emphasizing its importance for long-term code health.

# Practices

## DESIGN-ARRANGE-ACT-ASSERT-IMPLEMENT-REPEAT, AKA TDD

### 📝 What:

A software development method that requires writing tests before writing the code to facilitate testing and ensure its functionality. It is known as Test Driven Development, or TDD.

### ❓ Why:

TDD has many benefits that make it a valuable approach to software development. It has proven its usefulness through the years. Here are some of its strengths and how we could benefit by applying it:

- Higher Code Quality:

Writing tests before the actual implementation naturally forces us to think deeply about the requirements and design of the software. This results in well-structured code. A test represents the skeleton of the future implementation. That means we have to describe the problem through a test scenario, but we also need to think about the objects, the correlation between them, and the actions that are going to happen. That leads to a better design.

Since we must programmatically describe all the possible scenarios and create the objects (or mock them) we are completely aware of the overall structure of the upcoming code. This will lead to more modular, decoupled, and testable code, and reduce code repetition.

- Less Bugs:

All being said, the quality benefits lead to fewer bugs with a high test code coverage.

Writing tests first means that defects are identified early in the development process, making them easier and cheaper to fix. Following the approach, we will continuously run tests during development, and catch issues before they become deeply embedded in the codebase.

- Maintainability and Refactoring:

TDD promotes frequent refactoring without fear of introducing bugs due to the high percentage of code coverage. The test suite acts as a safety net, ensuring that changes made during refactoring do not break existing functionality.

- Faster Development:

Although writing tests first may seem to slow down development initially, it often results in faster overall development.

Tests act as a specification, making it easier to understand what the code should do and reducing the time spent on debugging.

- Clear and Documented Requirements:

TDD requires clear and specific tests, which can act as executable specifications for the software. This helps in better understanding the requirements and aligning the development process with the desired outcomes.

Test cases act as living documentation of the software's behavior. Developers can look at the test suite to understand how different parts of the system are supposed to work, even if there is no comprehensive documentation available.

## 🔧 How:

The framework for implementing TDD is widely advocated across many educational materials like books, articles, and videos. Here is the commonly described sequence of actions that will fulfill the approach:

1. Write the tests.
2. Run the tests to fail the assertions.
3. Implement the failing parts until the tests succeed.

I think there is a missing prerequisite here and I would add it as a step zero:

0. Create the initial design.

Design creation is needed to create appropriate test cases. That is the phase where you have to take a pen and a piece of paper, examine the requirements, and draw the architecture of the new feature. Only then, based on the outcome design you have created you can start with the first test and continue with the process.

# THE SECOND BRAIN, AKA PAIR PROGRAMMING

### 📝 What:

Pair programming is a development approach in which two developers work together at a single workstation on the same piece of code. One person, known as the "driver", writes the code, while the other, the "observer" or "navigator," reviews each line of code as it's typed. The roles can be swapped regularly to foster continuous collaboration and knowledge sharing.

Pair programming may seem unconventional at first, as it involves dedicating two developers to accomplish the work of one. However, the benefits it offers far outweigh the initial resource investment. Let's delve into the advantages of pair programming and why it's becoming a cornerstone of many successful software development teams.

### ❓ Why:

- Improved Code Quality:

One of the primary benefits of "the second brain" practice is improving code quality. When two minds collaborate on a problem, they bring different perspectives and experiences to the table. This often leads to early detection and resolution of bugs, logic errors, and potential design flaws.

What happens is that there is a constant code review during the development process. This helps maintain a high standard of code quality and ensures that best practices are followed consistently.

- Continuous Learning and Knowledge Sharing:

In a pair programming setup, developers continuously exchange ideas, share knowledge, and learn from one another. Junior developers benefit from the guidance and expertise of their more experienced counterparts, while senior developers can gain new insights from the fresh perspectives of their partners. This dynamic knowledge transfer leads to a more skilled and well-rounded team.

- Increased Collaboration and Communication:

Pair programming fosters strong communication and collaboration between team members. Developers must articulate their thoughts, explain their approach, and justify their decisions in real-time. This open and ongoing dialogue helps prevent misunderstandings and miscommunications, promoting a smoother and more efficient development process.

- Quicker Problem Solving:

Tackling complex issues becomes more manageable with two minds working in tandem. When facing a challenging problem, pairs can brainstorm solutions and bounce ideas off each other. This collaboration often results in faster and more effective problem-solving than working individually.

- Team Morale and Cohesion:

Pair programming can boost team morale and cohesion. Developers feel more connected to their colleagues as they actively collaborate and support each other's efforts. This positive team dynamic can increase job satisfaction and overall team productivity.

## 🔧 How:

The next time you have a task to develop, ask for a colleague to sit next to you, or share the screen if you are going to do it online and give it a try.

Some recommendations though:

- If possible, try to do it in person. It will be much easier for both sides to share ideas, point with fingers, and brainstorm through the development process.

- Do not be shy or afraid of what the other person would think about your way of working. Do your thinking and development as it is most efficient for you and try to adapt to the other person.

- Do not hesitate to share your ideas.

- Ask your pair for his/her opinion on unclear matters.

- Change the roles from time to time. Do this step whenever you feel it is appropriate to be done. For example, it is not a good idea to follow a strict schedule.

# THE SECOND PAIR OF EYES, AKA CODE REVIEW

## 📝 What:

Code review is the systematic examination of another person's code implementation. The aim is to uphold high code quality standards, align with the company's criteria, ensure satisfactory performance and security measures, and ultimately confirm that the code effectively fulfills the intended business requirements.

It is a common learning process and a team effort to achieve a shared goal.

## ? **Why:**

Code reviews offer several crucial benefits to software development teams and the overall quality of the codebase. Here's why conducting code reviews is essential:

- Quality Assurance:

Code reviews help identify and rectify coding errors, bugs, and logic flaws before they reach production. This contributes to higher code quality and reduces the likelihood of defects slipping into the final product.

- Knowledge Sharing:

Code reviews allow team members to learn from each other's code. Developers can share insights, best practices, and coding techniques, fostering a culture of continuous learning. Remember that this knowledge sharing happens not only between Seniors and Juniors but among all team members. Everyone can learn from each other because we are all different people with different experiences, different preferences, different ways of thinking, and different knowledge. Even if you have decades in the field, you might learn something from a junior, either from a provocative and basic question, or from a simpler implementation than you would initially think of, or maybe you can see something new, that the green one has just learned in the university.

- Consistency:

Code reviews ensure that coding standards, naming conventions, and design patterns are adhered to consistently across the codebase. This consistency makes the codebase more maintainable and understandable.

- Performance Optimization:

Through code reviews, potential performance bottlenecks and inefficiencies can be identified and optimized early in the development process, leading to a more performant application.

- Security Enhancement:

Code reviews help identify security vulnerabilities and potential risks in the code. Addressing these issues early can prevent security breaches and data leaks.

- Collaboration:

Code reviews encourage collaboration and teamwork. Team members can provide constructive feedback, suggest improvements, and collectively work towards producing the best possible code.

- Conflict Resolution:

Disagreements about design decisions or coding approaches can be resolved through code reviews. Team members can discuss and align on the best solutions, promoting a harmonious work environment.

- Ownership and Accountability:

Developers take ownership of their code when they know it will be reviewed. This can lead to a sense of accountability and responsibility for the quality of their work.

- Codebase Understanding:

Reviewing code written by others helps team members gain a deeper understanding of the codebase's various parts, which can be especially valuable when making changes in the future.

- Risk Mitigation:

Catching issues early in the development process reduces the risk of encountering problems during testing or after deployment, leading to smoother development cycles and fewer last-minute fixes.

- Continuous Improvement:

By regularly reviewing code, teams can identify recurring issues, pain points, and areas for improvement. This drives a culture of continuous improvement and helps refine development practices.

- Long-Term Maintenance:

Code that has undergone thorough reviews is typically easier to maintain over time. Future developers can more easily understand the code's intent and functionality.

Remember that the review process could only have a positive impact. Its aim is purely to produce a better product. Finger-pointing has nothing to do with this. If someone abuses this practice to make other people feel bad about their work or to put others down, then those individuals need to take leadership and team-oriented courses and be kept under a close eye from their managers.

Be yourself, be creative, and don't be afraid to provide unpopular solutions if you think they are better than the ones broadly used in your project.

## ✖ How:

Let me give you 10 steps for a good code review that you should keep in mind every time you are validating your colleague's implementation.

**3.** Understand the problem.

Begin by familiarizing yourself with the specific problem the implementation aims to solve. Review the acceptance criteria and discuss them with the Business Analyst (BA) and the developer who has created the code you are reviewing, to gain a complete understanding.

**4.** Coding conventions.

Ensure that the code adheres to established coding conventions for the programming language being used. Consistency in coding guidelines enhances readability and maintainability.

**5.** Naming conventions.

Pay attention to proper naming conventions. Consistent and meaningful naming contributes to code readability and should not be overlooked.

**6.** Look for unneeded code.

Look for any unused or orphaned code fragments, methods, or classes. Avoid keeping commented-out (so-called *zombie*) code - rely on source control for historical references.

**7.** Test coverage.

Evaluate the test coverage of the newly added functionality. Run all tests to confirm their successful execution, although this might also be part of the Continuous Integration (CI) process.

**8.** Design Considerations.

Assess whether the chosen design approach aligns with the project's context. Consider the suitability of design patterns and their fit within the project's architecture.

**9.** Think about the big picture and how this solution fits in it.

Examine how the solution fits within the broader project ecosystem. Check for potential impacts on existing components and overall project stability.

**10.** Think about alternative ways of implementation.

Consider alternative implementation approaches. Evaluate multiple options to determine the best fit for the project's requirements.

**11.** Is it Production-Ready and safe?

Analyze potential risks and assess whether the changes could potentially break existing functionality. Ensure the solution aligns with the project's goals and objectives.

Verify the implementation is production-ready and aligned with the company's release policies.

Imagine the following possible scenario: several projects are dependent on each other, and several of them have new changes. The company's release policy doesn't allow the simultaneous release of every library at the same time. Furthermore, no downtime is acceptable.

As a code reviewer, you should think about the described situation and constraints, consider the release order, check whether the implementation follows a release-safe strategy that will not affect the system's availability, and look for any other potential dangers or discrepancies that could lead to violations.

**12.** Is it understandable and simple enough?

K.I.S.S. and leave the ego behind.

# STEP-BY-STEP

The following practice can be applied to not-so-big technical implementations. However, even if you have a big feature to develop you can try to split it into smaller chunks and then implement the "Step-By-Step" technique.

## What:

It proposes a way of performing a particular task in phases until reaching the final result. In this particular technique, I propose three steps.

- Step 1 is about understanding the requirement and sketching the solution approach.

- Step 2 is to build logic by accomplishing the task in the easiest way for you.

- Step 3 is meant to improve the implementation of the previous step.

## ❓ Why:

You might be the kind of person who wants to provide a quality solution and loves your job as a software developer. However, sometimes it can be overwhelming, too time-consuming, or just plain difficult to dive into the perfect code implementation right away. Reading through the requirements and expecting the best result simultaneously can be hard to manage. You might feel discouraged, think you're not smart enough or get demotivated— which can even lead to burnout. But these feelings are misleading. It's completely normal to find it tough to visualize the entire solution with the best implementation from the get-go.

That's where the "Step-By-Step" technique comes in handy. Start by brainstorming ideas, then move on to an implementation that might not be perfect but works. Finally, apply all the good practices and optimizations you know are appropriate for your case.

This way, you'll be able to build the final product gradually, without putting too much stress on your mind and well-being.

## 🛠 How:

## Step 1

The first step is about brainstorming the approach.

Think about the problem and sketch your design somewhere - this will be the foundation of your work. Ensure you understand the requirements fully. Don't hesitate to ask as many questions as needed to get a clear picture of what is expected from a business or functional perspective.

Once you have a thorough understanding, grab your favorite brainstorming tool. Mine is a good old paper notebook, but you might prefer digital tools. Sketch your idea, write pseudo code, draw a mind map, create a diagram—whatever helps clarify your thoughts for the coding phase.

## Step 2

Next, turn your design into code. Don't worry about perfection here. The goal of this phase is not to craft the best-performing solution or implement perfect design patterns. Instead, focus on building a functional piece that meets the requirements.

Write your initial implementation and test all the possible cases you can think of to ensure it works correctly.

## Step 3

We reached the last step. It is all about quality, performance, and professionalism.

Many people stop at Step 2, sometimes even skipping a thorough Step 1. However, Step 3 is crucial for making your software stand out and for you to grow as a software engineer.

In this step, revisit your working solution and refine it until you are satisfied. Focus on performance: if you're dealing with an algorithm, ensure you've chosen the most efficient one for your particular case. Consider the SOLID principles and verify that your implementation adheres to them. Refactor if necessary to achieve satisfactory results.

Make sure your solution aligns with the overall project and fits within the ecosystem you're working in. Follow established guidelines and modify your solution to satisfy the project's agreed-upon approaches.

One very appropriate application of the mentioned approach is during a job interview. Especially when faced with algorithmic questions or specific problem-solving tasks.

## Example:

Imagine you have given the following question:

"You have 2 collections of numbers. Write a code to find the equal numbers from both collections."

### Step 1

Read the requirements as many times as you need to understand the task.

Ask clarifying questions. For example - "How big can be the biggest number?", "Can we have negative numbers?", "What would be the expected size of the collections?", "What would be the behavior on incorrect values (e.g. non-numbers in the collection)? Are incorrect values even possible? Should I check for those?", etc.

Asking these questions shows that you think critically and won't overlook details.

Once you have all the information, start brainstorming.

### Step 2

Write the implementation the easiest way you can think of. The most convenient thing in most cases is to try to solve the puzzle in your head, or on paper, the way your brain would do it in a real situation. Let's say you have the numbers written in front of you. Write down two collections with some random numbers. Naturally solve the puzzle and document your thinking process, then translate that logic into pseudocode or text. This makes it easier to follow your logic when you start coding.

Let's imagine that the first thing you can think of is the following algorithm and you start with the writing:

Algorithm 1: Initial idea - Brute Force Nested Loop

```
using System;
using System.Collections.Generic;

class Program
{
    static List<int> FindEqualNumbers(
        List<int> collection1, List<int> collection2)
    {
        List<int> equalNumbers = new List<int>();

        foreach (int num1 in collection1)
        {
            foreach (int num2 in collection2)
            {
                if (num1 == num2)
                {
                    equalNumbers.Add(num1);
                }
            }
        }

        return equalNumbers;
    }

    static void Main(string[] args)
    {
        List<int> collection1 = new List<int>
        {
            5, 2, 9, 1, 6
        };
        List<int> collection2 = new List<int>
        {
            1, 2, 6, 8, 9
        };
```

```
        List<int> equalNumbers =
            FindEqualNumbers(collection1, collection2);

        Console.WriteLine("Equal Numbers:");
        foreach (int num in equalNumbers)
        {
            Console.WriteLine(num);
        }
    }
}
```

This algorithm iterates through each number in the first collection and compares it with each in the second to find equal numbers.

## Step 3

Now that you have a working solution, you can relax a bit, right? The final step is about improving and showcasing your skills, intellect, and professionalism.

What you need to do is revisit your initial algorithm and analyze it:

Complexity:

Identify the complexity of the implementation.

Since you have 2 nested foreach loops, the time complexity is **O(n \* m)**, where n is the number of elements in the first collection and m is the number of elements in the second collection.

Space Complexity: O(1), as it only requires a constant amount of extra space.

Now, how would you improve that time complexity?

Take your time, and use whatever tools help you think. For me, paper and pen are always handy.

You can eventually come up with another implementation, for example, the following one, using a hash set:

Algorithm 2: Better Complexity - Hash Set

```
using System;
using System.Collections.Generic;

class Program
{
    static List<int> FindEqualNumbersFaster(
        List<int> collection1, List<int> collection2)
    {
        var numbersSet = new HashSet<int>(collection1);
        var equalNumbers = new List<int>();

        foreach (int num in collection2)
        {
            if (numbersSet.Contains(num))
            {
                equalNumbers.Add(num);
            }
        }

        return equalNumbers;
    }

    static void Main(string[] args)
    {
        var collection1 = new List<int>
        {
            5, 2, 9, 1, 6
        };
        var collection2 = new List<int>
        {
            1, 2, 6, 8, 9
        };

        var equalNumbers = FindEqualNumbersFaster(
            collection1, collection2);

        Console.WriteLine("Equal Numbers:");
        foreach (int num in equalNumbers)
        {
            Console.WriteLine(num);
        }
    }
}
```

This algorithm uses a hash set to store the numbers from one collection, then iterates through the second collection to check for equality.

Complexity:

Time Complexity: O(n + m), where n is the number of elements in the first collection and m is the number of elements in the second collection.

Space Complexity: O(n), where n is the number of elements in the first collection.

The performance difference between these two algorithms can be significant, especially for larger collections. Algorithm 2 (using a hash set) is more efficient as it has a linear time complexity compared to the quadratic time complexity of Algorithm 1 (brute force nested loop).

The choice of algorithm does depend on the size of the collections - for smaller collections, the difference might not be significant, but for larger collections, Algorithm 2 is a much preferable choice.

Not bad, isn't it?

The "Step-By-Step" technique could help you build an efficient solution by splitting the effort and focusing on one bit at a time.

*Note:

Always be creative and listen to your own needs. Feel free to modify the proposed approach to fit your style. If you feel you need more steps, go ahead and extend the Step-By-Step process. Make it your own by adding steps like researching different approaches or discussing your idea with a colleague for feedback. Create the perfect process for yourself and apply it whenever you need it.

# UBIQUITOUS LANGUAGE

### 📝 What:

Effective communication is paramount in software development. Misunderstandings, misinterpretations, and miscommunications can lead to costly errors and project delays. To mitigate these challenges, software engineers have adopted various practices, one of the most crucial being the concept of a "Ubiquitous Language."

This term is often associated with Domain-Driven Design (DDD). It represents a set of principles and practices in software development. Eric Evans uses it in his book "Domain-Driven Design: Tackling Complexity in the Heart of Software".

At its core, the Ubiquitous Language is a shared vocabulary that unifies the software development team, including developers, domain experts, and stakeholders. It's a language where terms and phrases have clear, consistent meanings that are universally understood within the project context.

### ❓ Why:

- Bridging the Communication Gap

In software development projects, different roles often speak different languages. Developers use technical jargon, domain experts use domain-specific terms, and stakeholders may have their own business language. This diversity can lead to misunderstandings and misalignments.

Ubiquitous Language acts as a bridge that connects these disparate languages. By establishing a common vocabulary, it ensures that all project participants communicate with precision and clarity.

- Improved Collaboration

Effective communication is the cornerstone of collaboration. When team members share a common language, they can collaborate more seamlessly. Developers can understand the requirements of domain experts, domain experts can comprehend technical constraints, and stakeholders can be confident that their needs are being accurately translated into code.

- Reduced Ambiguity

Ambiguity is the enemy of software development. Ambiguous language can lead to vague requirements, unclear specifications, and ultimately, software that doesn't meet the intended purpose. A Ubiquitous Language eliminates this ambiguity by providing a single, well-defined interpretation for each term or concept.

- Enhanced Problem Solving

In complex software projects, there are often intricate domain-specific challenges to overcome. A shared Ubiquitous Language empowers the development team to discuss these challenges with precision, ensuring that solutions are aligned with the project's true needs.

## 🔧 How:

Implementing a Ubiquitous Language in your software development project requires a structured approach:

1. Collaboration

Start by bringing all project stakeholders together for a collaborative discussion. This includes developers, domain experts, business analysts, and anyone else involved in the project. Encourage open dialogue to identify domain-specific terms and concepts.

Another approach would be for the implementation (development) team to listen closely during the project discussions, or reuse the same vocabulary as written in the stories, to identify the used terminology and proceed to point 2.

2. Create a Glossary

Compile all the terms, phrases, and concepts that arise into a glossary. Document each term along with its definition and usage within the project.

3. Consistent Usage

Ensure that all team members, including developers, adhere to the established vocabulary. Consistency is key; using Ubiquitous Language sparingly or inconsistently can lead to confusion.

4. Refinement

As the project progresses, revisit the glossary regularly. New terms may emerge, or existing definitions may need clarification. The Ubiquitous Language should evolve with the project's changing needs.

5. Documentation

Maintain comprehensive project documentation that includes the Ubiquitous Language glossary. This is a reference for all team members and can be invaluable for onboarding new team members.

# Design Patterns

This book's purpose is to familiarize you with the principles of software development. Principles and design patterns are closely related concepts that work together to guide and shape the creation of high-quality, maintainable, and effective software solutions. They provide different levels of guidance and abstraction in the software development process.

I have already mentioned several times about the design patterns, so it is worth at least having a brief description of them. That is what this chapter is dedicated to.

Design patterns are specific solutions to recurring design problems developers encounter during the software development process. These patterns are well-tested, reusable templates that provide proven ways to solve common architectural, structural, and behavioral challenges in software design.

They are more detailed and specific than software development principles. They offer concrete implementations and guidelines for solving particular design issues, such as how to structure classes and objects, manage relationships, handle interactions, and organize code to achieve desired goals.

The design patterns, also known as "Gang of Four" (GoF) design patterns, refer to a collection of 23 fundamental ones outlined in the book "Design Patterns: Elements of Reusable Object-Oriented Software." The book was written by Erich Gamma, Richard Helm, Ralph Johnson, and John Vlissides, collectively known as the "Gang of Four" or GoF.

*These patterns provide reusable solutions to common design problems* in object-oriented software development. The GoF patterns are categorized into three main types based on their purpose: *creational*, *structural*, and *behavioral*.

# CREATIONAL

Creational patterns focus on the process of object creation, providing flexible and controlled ways to create objects. They abstract the instantiation process, making it more dynamic and adaptable to different situations.

Examples of creational patterns include:

## Factory Method

Defines an interface for creating objects but delegates the instantiation to subclasses. This promotes loose coupling and allows for easy addition of new types.

- Use Cases:

- o GUI Frameworks: Creating different UI elements like buttons, text fields, and checkboxes through factory methods that follow a common interface.

- o Document Processing: Generating various document types (PDF, Word, HTML) using document factory methods.

- o Payment Gateways: Creating payment gateway instances based on the chosen payment method.

## Abstract Factory

Provides an interface for creating families of related or dependent objects without specifying their concrete classes. It supports creating objects with consistent behavior within a family.

- Use Cases:

  - o GUI Libraries: Creating related UI components like buttons, text fields, and menus that follow a common theme or style.

  - o Operating System APIs: Building platform-specific UI components and behaviors that follow the guidelines of the underlying operating system.

  - o Vehicle Manufacturing: Creating related objects for different vehicle parts, such as engines, tires, and seats.

## Singleton

The Singleton pattern ensures that a class has only one instance and provides a global access point to that instance. It is often used to control access to shared resources and centralize certain operations.

- Use Cases:

o Configuration Managers: Ensuring there's only one instance of a configuration manager that provides access to application settings.

o Logger: Having a single logger instance that captures and manages log messages throughout the application.

o Database Connection Pool: Creating a single pool of database connections that can be reused by different parts of the application.

## Builder

It separates the construction of a complex object from its representation, allowing step-by-step object creation. This is useful for creating objects with multiple optional components.

- Use Cases:

  o HTML Document Construction: Building complex HTML documents with various elements, styles, and attributes using a builder pattern.

  o Meal Ordering: Constructing complex meals with multiple components (main course, sides, drinks) in a flexible way.

  o Report Generation: Creating reports with varying content, formatting, and sections using a report builder.

## Prototype

It involves creating new objects by copying an existing prototype instance. This method is helpful when you need to create similar instances efficiently without the cost of full initialization.

- Use Cases:

- o Document Cloning: Generating new documents with similar content but minor differences based on a prototype.

- o Game Character Generation: Creating new game characters by copying an existing character prototype and customizing certain attributes.

- o User Profiles: Generating new user profiles by copying existing profiles and adjusting specific settings.

# STRUCTURAL

Structural patterns focus on organizing objects and classes to form larger structures while maintaining flexibility and efficiency. They help define relationships between objects and classes to achieve composition and reusability.

Examples of structural patterns include:

## Adapter

Converts the interface of a class into another interface clients expect, allowing classes with incompatible interfaces to work together. It allows objects with incompatible interfaces to work together by providing a wrapper that translates one interface into another. It enables objects with different interfaces to collaborate smoothly.

- • Use Cases:
  - o Legacy Integration: Integrating legacy systems or components with new systems that have different interfaces.

- o Third-Party Libraries: Making third-party libraries or APIs compatible with your codebase's interface.

- o Device Compatibility: Making software compatible with various devices or platforms by adapting their interfaces.

## Bridge

The Bridge pattern decouples an abstraction from its implementation, allowing both to vary independently. It separates the interface from the implementation to create a flexible structure.

- • Use Cases:

  - o Graphics Libraries: Creating a hierarchy of shapes with different drawing implementations (e.g., raster vs. vector).

  - o Database Drivers: Providing different database drivers with varying implementations for different databases.

  - o Remote Controls: Building remote controls that can work with different devices, like TVs and stereos.

## Composite

Composes objects into tree structures to represent part-whole hierarchies. Clients can treat individual objects and compositions of objects uniformly.

- • Use Cases:

  - o GUI Components: Constructing complex UI elements like windows, panels, and controls using a hierarchy of composite objects.

- File Systems: Representing files and directories as a composite structure to navigate a file system.

- Organizational Hierarchies: Modeling organizational structures with employees and departments as components.

## Decorator

Attaches additional responsibilities to objects dynamically, providing a flexible alternative to subclassing for extending functionality.

- Use Cases:

  - Text Formatting: Adding various formatting options (bold, italic, underline) to text without creating many subclasses.

  - Coffee Shop: Modifying coffee orders with extra ingredients or options without creating a separate class for each combination.

  - Vehicle Customization: Enhancing vehicles with additional features (GPS, leather seats) without creating numerous subclasses.

## Facade

The Facade pattern provides a unified interface to a set of interfaces in a subsystem. It simplifies complex systems and shields clients from the details of individual components.

- Use Cases:

  - API Wrappers: Creating simplified interfaces for complex APIs to make them more user-friendly.

o Operating System Interfaces: Offering a simplified interface to interact with complex operating system functions.

o Online Shopping: Providing a single interface for users to browse products, add items to a cart, and place orders.

## Flyweight

It focuses on efficiently sharing and reusing objects that have many similar properties or states. It aims to reduce memory usage and improve performance by sharing common data among multiple objects instead of duplicating it. This pattern is handy when dealing with a large number of small, similar objects that consume significant memory resources if created individually.

In the Flyweight pattern, objects are divided into intrinsic (shared) and extrinsic (unique) states. Intrinsic states are shared among multiple objects, while extrinsic states can vary between objects. By isolating and sharing the intrinsic states, the Flyweight pattern minimizes memory consumption and allows more efficient utilization of resources.

- Use Cases:
  - o Text Editors: Sharing common font and formatting objects across multiple instances of text in a document.
  - o Graphic Design: Reusing colors, patterns, and other resources in graphic design software to reduce memory usage.
  - o Game Development: Managing sprites and resources in games to optimize memory consumption.

## Proxy

Provides a surrogate or placeholder for another object. It acts as an intermediary, controlling access to the real object and allowing additional functionality to be added when needed. Proxies can be used to implement lazy loading, access control, logging, caching, and more.

By using proxies, developers can enhance the functionality of an object without modifying its core implementation. Proxies are especially useful when dealing with objects that are resource-intensive or need controlled access.

- Use Cases:
    - Virtual Proxies: Delaying the creation of resource-intensive objects until they're needed.
    - Remote Proxies: Representing remote objects to enable communication between local and remote systems.
    - Access Control: Restricting access to sensitive operations or resources by using proxy objects.

# BEHAVIORAL

Behavioral patterns focus on communication between objects and classes, facilitating collaboration and interaction among different system components.

Examples of behavioral patterns include:

## Chain of Responsibility

The Chain of Responsibility pattern creates a chain of handler objects, where each handler decides whether to process a request or pass it to the next handler in the chain. It avoids coupling the sender of a request to its receiver.

- Use Cases:

    - Logging Systems: Processing log messages at different levels (debug, info, error) by passing them through a chain of handlers.

    - User Input Handling: Handling user input events in GUI applications through a series of event handlers.

## Command

It encapsulates a request as an object, allowing for the parameterization of clients with different requests, the queuing of requests, and the logging of their execution.

- Use Cases

    - GUI Actions: Implementing actions in a GUI application that can be executed, undone, or redone.

    - Remote Control Systems: Creating remote controls for devices that allow users to execute commands (e.g., TV remote).

## Interpreter

Defines a language's grammar and provides an interpreter to evaluate sentences in the language. It's used to create domain-specific languages or handle grammatical structures.

- Use Cases:

    - Query Languages: Parsing and evaluating queries in databases or search engines.

o Regular Expressions: Interpreting and matching patterns in text using regular expression engines.

## Iterator

It provides a way to access the elements of a collection sequentially without exposing its underlying representation. It decouples the collection from its traversal logic.

- Use Cases:

  o Data Structures: Implementing iterators for collections like lists, arrays, and trees.

  o File Navigation: Traversing files and directories in file systems using iterators.

## Mediator

The Mediator pattern defines an object that centralizes communication among a set of objects, reducing direct interactions between them. It promotes loose coupling and simplifies complex communication scenarios.

- Use Cases:

  o Chat Applications: Managing communication between multiple users in a chat room.

  o Air Traffic Control: Coordinating the communication between air traffic controllers and planes.

## Memento:

Captures an object's internal state and stores it externally, allowing it to be restored to that state later. It's useful for implementing undo functionality.

- Use Cases:

  o Text Editors: Implementing undo and redo functionality in text editors.

  o Game States: Saving and restoring game states in video games.

## Observer

This pattern defines a dependency between objects so that when one object changes its state, all its dependents are notified and updated automatically.

- Use Cases:

  o UI Updates: Keeping UI elements synchronized with changes in underlying data models.

  o Stock Market Updates: Notifying investors when stock prices change.

## State

Allows an object to change its behavior when its internal state changes. It's beneficial when an object's behavior depends on multiple states.

- Use Cases:

  o Vending Machines: Implementing different behaviors for a vending machine based on its current state (e.g., "Has Coin," "Dispensing").

  o Document Editors: Switching between editing and viewing modes in document editors.

## Strategy

It defines a family of algorithms that encapsulates each algorithm and makes them interchangeable. It allows clients to switch between different algorithms without altering the client's code.

- Use Cases:
  - Sorting Algorithms: Providing different sorting strategies (e.g., quick sort, merge sort) for sorting collections.
  - Payment Methods: Implement various payment strategies (credit card, PayPal) to process payments.

## Template Method

Defines the structure of an algorithm but lets subclasses override specific steps. It creates a common algorithm structure while allowing variations in some steps.

- Use Cases:
  - Document Generation: Creating templates for generating different types of documents (e.g., reports, invoices).
  - Online Ordering: Defining a template for order processing with variations in payment and shipping methods.

## Visitor

It lets you add further operations to objects without modifying them. It separates the algorithms from the objects on which they operate.

- Use Cases:

  - Document Processors: Applying different operations (e.g., printing, formatting) to elements of a document hierarchy.

  - AST Analysis: Analyzing abstract syntax trees in compilers or interpreters with varying operations of visitor.

These design patterns have become fundamental building blocks for designing robust, maintainable, and reusable software systems. By understanding and applying these patterns appropriately, developers can solve recurring design challenges efficiently and create well-structured, adaptable, and high-quality software.

# Anti-Principles: The Dark Side of Software Development

Understanding the art of software development isn't just about embracing best practices. It is also about recognizing the pitfalls that can lead us astray. In this chapter, we delve into the world of "Anti-Principles" – practices so wrong and harmful that they serve as cautionary tales. Picture a bag of smelly *durians*, each representing a blunder that can spoil your software endeavors.

Our journey through these Anti-Principles is not merely an exercise in finger-pointing but a valuable opportunity to learn from others' missteps. By understanding what not to do, we reinforce the significance of the good practices outlined in earlier chapters. So, brace yourself for a revealing exploration of common mistakes and misguided approaches that, with a little awareness, you can steer clear of in your software development journey.

Are you ready to uncover the unpleasant truths and ensure that your software projects remain free from the stench of failure? Let's begin then.

## REVERSE ENGINEERING

A principle that encourages programmers to write code that is difficult for consumers to use, extend, or understand. In some cases, it could even be difficult to decompile or reverse engineer. This is achieved using complex code obfuscators or encryption.

While there are cases where this is required, sometimes people decide to apply unneeded restrictions or over-protect internal libraries.

If this is needed, then appropriate documentation should be created. Every application, framework, or module is created to be used and to serve certain needs. If there is a need to protect the outcome in such a way, then most probably the code will be exposed publicly, or in a secured environment, or the executables or libraries will be used by another team, etc. In such examples, the product must be described with the following documentation:

- Usage Documentation:

This type of documentation should provide clear and concise instructions on how to use the code, library, or framework. It can include code samples, API references, and examples of common use cases.

- Design Documentation:

Detailed design documentation explains the architecture, design decisions, and the overall structure of the codebase. It helps developers understand the rationale behind the code's organization and helps maintainers make informed modifications.

- API Documentation:

If your code exposes an API (Application Programming Interface), thorough API documentation is essential. It should describe the functions, classes, and methods available, along with their parameters, return values, and usage examples.

- Security Documentation:

If code protection is a concern, security documentation should outline the security measures implemented within the code. It can describe encryption algorithms, authentication mechanisms, and any other security-related information.

- Deployment Documentation:

When the code is meant to be deployed in specific environments or configurations, documentation should guide users through the deployment process. This may include system requirements, installation steps, and configuration settings.

- Troubleshooting and Debugging Guides:

In case users encounter issues while using the code, troubleshooting guides can help them identify and resolve problems. Include common error messages and their solutions.

- Version History and Change Logs:

Keep a record of code changes over time. Document major updates, bug fixes, and enhancements in version history and change logs. This helps users stay informed about improvements and potential compatibility issues.

- Licensing and Usage Rights:

Clarify the licensing terms and usage rights associated with the code. Users should know how to use the code legally and what restrictions, if any, apply.

- Examples and Tutorials:

Provide real-world examples and tutorials that demonstrate the code's capabilities. This can help users learn how to use the code effectively.

- Performance and Optimization Guidelines:

If performance is a concern, offer guidance on optimizing and fine-tuning the code for specific use cases.

- Code Annotations and Comments:

Within the code itself, use comments and annotations to explain complex logic, algorithms, or any non-obvious implementation details.

## CODE NOSTALGIA

This principle recommends using outdated technologies and programming languages with a small community of programmers. This leads to a nostalgic effect when working on a project.

One example would be to use old programming technologies to build something modern. One of the many examples is using COBOL in Modern Web Development.

COBOL, originally developed in the late 1950s, was a powerful language for business applications, especially on mainframe systems. While it is still in use today, especially in financial institutions and government agencies, its application in modern web development is nearly nonexistent. A project that chooses COBOL for web backend development may invoke a nostalgic feel, especially among seasoned developers, but it will inevitably face severe limitations:

- Limited Talent Pool: Finding developers proficient in COBOL is increasingly challenging as newer languages dominate the curriculum and job market.

- Integration Issues: COBOL was not designed for modern web protocols and standards, leading to potential integration hurdles with contemporary technologies like RESTful services, JSON, and OAuth.

- Development Speed: Developing and maintaining web applications in COBOL can be significantly slower compared to using modern languages like JavaScript, Python, Go, or .NET.

Using a modern framework like .NET, specifically ASP.NET Core, offers numerous advantages:

- Improved Productivity: Features such as strong typing, a rich set of libraries, and a comprehensive development environment (Visual Studio) significantly enhance developer productivity.

- Cross-Platform Compatibility: ASP.NET Core is cross-platform, running on Windows, macOS, and Linux, which is essential for modern cloud-based applications.

- Robust Ecosystem: The .NET ecosystem provides integrated solutions for frontend frameworks, cloud integrations, and a highly active community, making it easier to find support, resources, and developers.

Another common example is when an older syntax is used when the new versions of the language or the framework provide new guidelines and syntax sugars that could help productivity and readability. It is a matter of team discussions and following agreed standards.

## MAGIC NUMBERS

This is a principle that encourages the use of numbers such as 42, 777, and 666 instead of constants or variables for easier memorization and understanding of the code.

I'm sure everyone has done or at least seen those in the code. They are like little aphids, standing there in your beautiful code garden, sucking the juice of your flower leaves.

What I mean is that when I look at such code and see those magic numbers, I don't have any idea how to interpret them and if I need to update the code there, I will not know whether I am going to break the business logic or not. We should write obvious, predictable, and understandable code.

If we need to hard-code some static, constant values, then it is better to do it properly:

- Create the necessary place where all constants will persist.
- Create the appropriate access level.
- Give them meaningful names.

- Document those if needed - write code comments or dedicate an article describing the constants.

- Double-check with the team to come up with the best scenario and, if possible, avoid the hard coding.

# NO COMMENTS

The principle of lack of comments encourages programmers not to write comments in the code, even if it is difficult to understand what the code does.

The general rule is to write a simple and easy-to-understand code that is self-explanatory and doesn't need any additional explanation. However, there are some situations in which a specific business logic is unclear to everyone, especially for new team members. Also, we could use domain terminology to represent the objects (refer to Ubiquitous Language (p. 120)). In those situations, some comments in the code can be useful.

People who adhere to the principle in question are not willing to write comments at all. In some cases, even they alone cannot understand the code they wrote some time ago. Without comments or documentation will slow them down with further program extension and maintenance.

# TOO MANY COMMENTS

This one stands on the opposite side of the previous anti-principle. It speaks for adding comments for almost every single line of code.

This can happen due to several reasons:

- The code is too complex and hard to understand.

    o The fix for this is extensively explained in this book.

- The developer misunderstood the idea of a self-explanatory code base.

    o Following good practices will prevent the need for too many comments.

- There is no technical documentation anywhere and the developers decide to explain everything inside the source code.

    o Dedicate a place where the project documentation resides. It can be a wiki page or even a documentation file in the source code repository.

- Employees' performance is measured by code quantity (lines of code).

    o It sounds like a joke, but it is not. Some companies use such performance evaluation metrics. This indicator doesn't show anything about how the person is performing. As we already stated in YAGNI (You Aren't Gonna Need It) (p. 70) - every line of code is a liability. So, I would say that the approach should be reversed. If the employee meets the expectations and provides what is being asked, writing fewer lines of code (than expected) is even better.

    o Do not fall into such bad management traps and be efficient.

    o Always prefer quality over quantity.

# COPY-PASTE

A principle that recommends programmers to copy and paste ready-made code from other projects instead of writing new code. This can lead to code duplication and difficulties in future maintenance.

I am not against this approach. But rather be conscious and carefully double-check whether you can improve something. Beware of blindly reusing another's or even your own code.

Alternatives to the "Copy-Paste" Anti-Pattern:

- Create Reusable Functions or Methods:

Instead of copying code, encapsulate common logic in reusable functions or methods. This promotes code reusability and ensures that changes or updates are made in a single location.

- Use Inheritance and Polymorphism:

In object-oriented programming, inheritance and polymorphism are leveraged to create a base class with shared functionality. Subclasses can then extend, or override methods as needed.

- Implement Design Patterns:

Explore design patterns (p. 123) such as the Singleton pattern, Factory pattern, or Strategy pattern to address common coding scenarios in a modular and reusable way.

- Library or Framework Usage:

When applicable, use libraries, frameworks, or third-party packages that provide pre-built solutions for common tasks or functionalities. This reduces the need for custom code.

- Refactor Code:

If you discover duplicated code in your codebase, take the time to refactor it into a single, reusable component. This improves code maintainability and reduces the risk of future duplication.

- Code Reviews and Best Practices:

Encourage code reviews within your development team to identify instances of code duplication. Establish best practices and coding guidelines that discourage the "Copy-Paste" approach.

In conclusion, avoiding the "Copy-Paste" anti-pattern and striving for code reusability, modularity, and maintainability is essential for building high-quality software. By adopting these alternatives and emphasizing good coding practices, developers can reduce technical debt, enhance code readability, and improve the overall efficiency of software development projects.

# OBFUSCATED NAMING

This principle recommends the use of complex and disproportionate variable and function names to make it difficult for other programmers to understand the code.

Every person has their own preferences. Some are pretty creative and show their creativity in the object names as well. Whatever we like, it is advisable to give the objects meaningful names. They should follow several criteria:

- Should be close to the domain (refer to Ubiquitous Language (p. 120)).

- Should describe or at least point us in the right direction of what their functional purpose is,

- Should follow an agreed naming convention common for the language and the team.

# GIANT MONOLITHIC

A principle that encourages creating large and complex monolithic applications that include all functions and components in one project. This can lead to bloated code and difficulty maintaining and extending the application.

There are several reasons why this is problematic:

- Maintenance Challenges:

Monolithic applications tend to be tightly coupled; thus it is difficult to make changes or updates to specific parts of the system without affecting others. This can lead to a high maintenance burden over time.

- Scalability Issues:

Monolithic applications may struggle to scale effectively. As the application grows, it becomes increasingly challenging to allocate resources and scale individual components independently. This can result in performance bottlenecks.

- Testing Complexity:

Testing a monolithic application can be complex and time-consuming. It's challenging to isolate and test individual components, which can hinder the ability to identify and fix bugs.

- Team Collaboration:

Large monolithic codebases can make collaboration among development teams more difficult. Multiple teams working on different application parts may inadvertently introduce conflicts and compatibility issues.

- Innovation Constraints:

Monolithic architectures can stifle innovation. It can be challenging to adopt new technologies, frameworks, or programming languages within a monolithic codebase because changes may have widespread impacts.

Alternatives to the "Giant Monolithic" approach include adopting more modern architectural patterns:

- Microservices:

Break down the application into smaller, independently deployable services, each responsible for a specific function. This promotes scalability, maintainability, and flexibility.

- Service-Oriented Architecture (SOA):

Like microservices, SOA divides the application into services, but it can be less granular. It emphasizes the use of well-defined interfaces for communication between services.

- Modular Architecture:

Organize the application into modules or components, each with a specific responsibility. These modules can be developed and maintained separately, promoting code reusability.

- Containerization:

Use containerization technologies like Docker to package and deploy individual components or services. This simplifies deployment and ensures consistency across different environments.

- Serverless Computing:

Consider serverless architectures where code is executed in response to events without the need to manage server infrastructure. This can simplify development and reduce operational overhead.

- Event-Driven Architecture:

Design the application to respond to events or messages, allowing for decoupled communication between components. This can enhance scalability and flexibility.

In summary, avoiding the "Giant Monolithic" approach in favor of more modular, decoupled, and scalable architectural patterns can lead to more maintainable, efficient, and innovative software systems. These alternatives can also improve code organization, facilitate testing, and improve collaboration between development teams.

# THE FUNNY GUY

Also commonly encountered, this principle involves having someone on the team with a greater sense of humor, or at least they think so. As a result of this self-deception, many objects have strange names, names of comic book characters, mythical creatures, etc.

It might be fun, however, here's why I consider it a problematic practice:

- Code Readability:

Using humorous or unconventional names for objects, variables, or functions can significantly reduce code readability. Other team members, especially newcomers, may struggle to understand the purpose and functionality of these elements, leading to confusion and increased learning curves.

- Maintainability:

In the long term, maintaining code with quirky or non-standard names can become challenging. Excessive documentation or comments to explain the humor may be required, adding complexity to the codebase.

- Professionalism:

While a sense of humor can enhance team dynamics, overly humorous or unprofessional naming conventions may not align with the desired level of professionalism in software development. It is important to balance a relaxed work environment and maintaining a degree of formality.

- Collaboration:

Collaboration among team members is vital in software development. Using unconventional or humorous naming conventions may hinder effective communication and collaboration, as team members might spend extra time deciphering the meaning behind such names.

- Future Maintainability:

As software projects evolve and new team members join, the initial humor behind naming conventions may be lost or misinterpreted. This can lead to confusion and potential errors when maintaining or extending the codebase. Instead of this, you should:

- Use descriptive naming.

- Establish and adhere to coding standards and naming conventions within the development team.

- If humorous or unconventional explanations are needed, consider using comments or documentation outside the code itself.

- Encourage team bonding activities or breaks to inject humor and maintain a positive work environment. Balancing professionalism with a sense of fun can foster creativity and collaboration without compromising code quality.

## JOB SECURITY

This is somewhat the opposite of the KISS principle.

It recommends doing every implementation in the most complex way, using uncommon naming conventions, and doing it by choosing the hardest and unmaintainable approach. Such code usually is not readable at all and to understand a certain piece of logic you will probably need at least twice the time you would normally need for such a thing.

This anti-principle could be done for several reasons.

- One of those is that someone wants to play it smart, which makes everything look ultra-complex. A lot of junior developers will look at that code and will think the guy who wrote it is a pure genius. Let me tell you something - the most genius things are the simple things. It is much smarter (and often harder) to end up with a simple solution, rather than a complex one.

- Some people also apply it to their implementation to make themselves irreplaceable, as the name suggests. They want to be sure that if something happens to that software or if the business needs to extend it, they will be the only ones who can possibly handle it.

I think there is no need to say why this way of working is toxic and really bad practice in multiple important aspects. The justifications for it are mere illusions, and eventually, everyone will realize the harsh reality. The impact will undoubtedly be negative, affecting both the developers and the project.

Let me give you one example from my experience.

I've been working on a project where the main developer, who has built the system from the ground up, has chosen a specific library. This sounds totally fine, right? Except that the library was one he had personally developed. He made it open-source and freely available, which seemed like a positive move at first. However, when he left the company, the situation turned problematic. He didn't violate any license or internal rule, but the lack of thorough documentation and unfamiliarity with the library among the remaining team members made maintenance and extension incredibly challenging.

Then, guess what? The team was unhappy and frustrated. They frequently made excuses when change requests came in and constantly needed to explain why additional time was required to implement new features.

Be mindful and stop that practice as soon as you notice it.

## ONE TO RULE THEM ALL

One to Rule Them All principle warns against the common practice of consolidating an excessive amount of logic into a single file. While this approach may initially seem convenient, it often results in unintended consequences, including tightly coupled code and a convoluted, hard-to-maintain codebase that resembles a plate of tangled spaghetti.

I would assert that various manifestations of this anti-pattern are among the most frequently encountered issues in project implementations. In general, there are a couple of reasons leading to the application of this bad practice:

- Lack of Knowledge:

In some cases, developers may not be aware of alternative approaches to improve code structure. They may lack the experience to recognize the potential problems that tightly coupled code can introduce.

- Short-Term Thinking:

Alternatively, developers might opt for this approach to save time and effort in the short term. They acknowledge the potential issues and possible solutions but choose expediency over long-term code maintainability. If we decide to work in an energy-saving regime, we effectively defer the problems to future developers or iterations of the project.

Not surprisingly, software engineering is a creative process in which we engineer something—we create the architecture.

Skipping the initial design phase resembles constructing a building without a solid foundation. It might seem reasonable initially, but it leaves your creation vulnerable to instability, inefficiency, and future complications. The architectural design phase lays the groundwork for a robust, scalable, and maintainable software system. It's where we anticipate challenges, plan for extensibility, and ensure that our solutions align with project goals.

The solution is simple - the next time you start a task, do not start straight away and write the code even before reading the story.

Instead, you can do the following:

- Read it carefully and clear all the functional questions with the businesspeople.
- Create the design on paper, with your favorite drawing tool, or, if it is really small, in your head only.
- Do the coding part after you have the clean design idea.

# The End... Is Not Here

The truth is that applying good principles and working with productive and useful practices is a never-ending story. Furthermore, the learning phase is a continuous process ending only after our last breath.

In this book, I have tried to share any information and tips that I believe are important. During my career I have changed multiple working environments, collaborating with different teams and working within numerous internal structures, rules, and cultures. In some situations, I have chosen good approaches, in others I have made mistakes or not-so-efficient decisions. However, the important thing here is the learning phase and trying to extract as much useful information as possible. Some, or maybe most things, are learned the hard way. I have spent many hours trying to solve difficult problems. There have been times when I've worked overtime to get out of tough situations, enduring stress and exerting extreme effort. I guess this is expected and normal to happen from time to time. However, I want to emphasize that I tried to identify and extract why those things happen and what can be done to prevent any excess effort and uncomfortable, unpleasant moments in this creative, intelligent, and exciting profession. These thoughts motivated me to start writing books that will ultimately help everyone with a passion for professional software development craftsmanship in their heart. I have extracted important principles and have often seen that violating them leads to problems and results in excessive time and effort.

Modifying your mindset and working habits to incorporate the best practices mentioned in this book will have a profound positive impact on your satisfaction, professionalism, growth, self-esteem, and confidence.

You will be amazed at how daily tasks will become a pleasant and anticipated activity. Giving the best of yourself will grant you satisfaction and an enjoyable and productive life. Be curious, do not stop learning, and be proud of your creations.

# Recap and Self-Assessment

Creating professional software sometimes requires a lot of effort, however the result would be quite fulfilling. This chapter summarizes everything we discussed and evaluates your adherence to the principles and practices discussed throughout this book. Consider it both - a recap and a checklist for self-improvement.

## CORE PRINCIPLES

1. S.O.L.I.D.

   - Single Responsibility Principle (SRP):

     o Does each class in your codebase have only one reason to change?

   - Open/Closed Principle (OCP):

- o Are your classes and modules open for extension but closed for modification?

- Liskov Substitution Principle (LSP):

  - o Can subclasses replace their base classes without altering the correctness of the program?

- Interface Segregation Principle (ISP):

  - o Are your interfaces small and client-specific instead of large and general-purpose?

- Dependency Inversion Principle (DIP):

  - o Do high-level modules depend on abstractions, not on low-level modules?

2. DRY (Don't Repeat Yourself)

   - Are there no repetitive patterns or duplicate code blocks in your codebase?

   - Is common functionality abstracted to be reusable?

3. KISS (Keep It Simple, Stupid)

   - Is your codebase free of unnecessary complexity?

   - Are your solutions the simplest ones that can work?

4. YAGNI (You Aren't Gonna Need It)

   - Are you avoiding speculative generality and building only what's required currently?

5. Composition over Inheritance

   - Do you prefer composition to inheritance to enhance code flexibility and reusability?

6. Convention over Configuration (CoC)

- Are you leveraging known conventions to reduce the need for extensive configurations and boilerplate code?

7. Separation of Concerns
   - Is your code modularized, with a clear separation of different functionalities?

   - Do your classes and functions focus on a single concern?

8. Borrow and Improve

   - Are you learning from existing solutions and continuously looking for ways to improve them?

## PRACTICES

1. Test-Driven Development (TDD)

   - Are you writing unit tests first before developing the actual code?

   - Do you rely on tests to guide your implementation and design decisions?

2. Pair Programming

   - Are you collaborating with a partner to write code to enhance quality and share knowledge?

   - Do you regularly switch between driving and navigating during pair programming sessions?

3. Code Reviews

   - Is your code reviewed by peers to catch issues early and share expertise?

   - Do you actively participate in the review process for others' code as well?

# DESIGN PATTERNS

1. Creational Patterns

   - Which patterns are you using to manage object creation effectively?

2. Structural Patterns

   - Are you applying patterns like Adapter, Composite, and Decorator to define relationships between entities?

3. Behavioral Patterns

   - Think of an example from your work or education experience of how the management of object interaction and responsibilities are handled. Did you come across a pattern like Strategy, Observer, or Command?

# ANTI-PRINCIPLES: AVOIDING THE DARK SIDE

1. Reverse Engineering

   - Are you avoiding unoriginal and quick fixes that substitute understanding with mimicry?

2. Code Nostalgia

   - Are you cautious of clinging to outdated methods without reevaluation?

3. Magic Numbers

   - Does your code avoid using hard-coded numbers, employing named constants or configurations instead?

4. Comment Misuse

   - Are your comments meaningful and not overly verbose?

- Do you write self-explanatory code that minimizes the need for comments?

5. Copy-Paste

   - Are you reusing code through proper abstraction rather than simple copying?

6. Obfuscated Naming

   - Do you use clear and meaningful variables, methods, and class names?

7. Giant Monolithic

   - Is your code broken down into manageable, small modules rather than massive monolithic blocks?

8. The Funny Guy

   - Is your code free of jokes and personal quirks that compromise professionalism and readability?

9. Job Security via Complexity

   - Do you avoid writing overly complex code that only you can understand?

10. One to Rule Them All

   - Are there no overbearing classes or methods that attempt to handle every possible scenario?

Final Thoughts

Self-assessment is a continuous process. Regularly evaluate your work, attention, and attitude toward these principles and practices. Strive for improvement, be open to feedback, and never stop learning. Adaptation and growth are key to becoming a proficient software developer.

Good luck and keep coding clean!

# Good Resources

Here is a small list of must-read titles, laying the ground for quality software development. Even though some of the examples and advice seem outdated, the main concept stays the same through time.

- Eric Evans - "Domain-Driven Design: Tackling Complexity in the Heart of Software"

- Erich Gamma, John Vlissides, Richard Helm, Ralph Johnson - "Design Patterns: Elements of Reusable Object-Oriented Software"

- Eric Freeman, Elisabeth Robson, Bert Bates, Kathy Sierra - "Head first design patterns"

- Roy Osherove - "The art of unit testing"

- Simon Brown - "Software architecture for developers"

- Robert Cecil Martin - "Clean Code" and "The Clean Coder"

- John Sonmez - "The Complete Software Developer's Career Guide"

- Joshua Kerievsky - "Refactoring to pattern"

- Martin Fowler - "Refactoring:Improving the Design of Existing Code"

"Any fool can write code that a computer can understand. Good programmers write code that humans can understand."

- Martin Fowler,
*Refactoring: Improving the Design of Existing Code*

# About the Author

My name is Svilen Peev, and I am from Bulgaria. I currently take the role of .NET Development Lead, having over 15 years of professional software development experience. Throughout my career, I have focused primarily on the Microsoft technology stack, working extensively with .NET, C#, and T-SQL. Additionally, I have experience with front-end technologies such as JavaScript, ReactJS, and Angular, among others.

As a seasoned developer, I have led numerous successful projects and have continuously advocated for best coding practices and innovative solutions. My dedication to continuous learning and improvement has earned me respect in my professional community.

Outside of my professional life, I am a devoted husband and father of two wonderful children. Balancing my career with family life inspires and motivates me to excel in my profession.

Writing "LIVE THE CODE: Programming Principles and Practices" was motivated by my belief that mastering essential software development principles is crucial for building high-quality, maintainable, and efficient software. I hope to share my knowledge and experiences with fellow developers to help them achieve excellence in their work.

Feel free to connect with me on LinkedIn:

https://www.linkedin.com/in/svilen-peev/.